Mental Toughness for Teen Athletes, Post COVID-19

Easy Strategies to Boost Fitness, Rebuild Your Physical Stamina and Reach Your Peak Performance in Only 4O Minutes per Day

Timothy Law

© Copyright 2024 Tim Law - All rights reserved.

The content contained within this book may not be reproduced, duplicated, or transmitted without direct written permission from the author or the publisher.

Under no circumstances will any blame or legal responsibility be held against the publisher, or author, for any damages, reparation, or monetary loss due to the information contained within this book. Either directly or indirectly. You are responsible for your own choices, actions, and results.

Legal Notice:

This book is copyright protected. This book is only for personal use. You cannot amend, distribute, sell, use, quote, or paraphrase any part of the content within this book without the consent of the author or publisher.

Disclaimer Notice:

Please note that the information contained within this document is for educational and entertainment purposes only. All effort has been executed to present accurate, up-to-date, reliable, and complete information. No warranties of any kind are declared or implied. Readers acknowledge that the author is not engaging in the rendering of legal, financial, medical, or professional advice. The content within this book has been derived from various sources. Please consult a licensed professional before attempting any techniques outlined in this book.

By reading this document, the reader agrees that under no circumstances is the author responsible for any losses, direct or indirect, which are incurred as a result of the use of the information contained within this document, including, but not limited to, — errors, omissions, or inaccuracies.

Contents

Foreword	V
Introduction	IX
1. The New Normal for Teen Athletes	1
1.1 Navigating the Shift: Sports in a Post-Covid World	
1.2 From Isolation to Integration: Rebuilding Team Dynamics	
1.3 The Psychological Impact of Missing Key Competitions	
2. Mental Health and Wellness Post-Covid	17
2.1 Recognizing Post-COVID-19 Anxiety and Its Effects on Performance	
2.2 Strategies for Managing Depression	
2.3 The Role of Sleep in Mental and Physical Recovery	
2.4 Nutrition for the Mind: Eating for Mental Toughness	
3. Core Principles of Resilience for Athletes	25
3.1 Understanding Resilience: More than Just Grit	
3.2 Setting and Adjusting Goals in Uncertain Times	
3.3 Embracing Vulnerability as Strength	
3.4 Cultivating a Growth Mindset Amidst Setbacks	
4. Practical Strategies for Enhanced Mental Toughness	35
4.1 Daily Habits for Stronger Mental Fortitude	
4.2 Visualization Techniques for Peak Performance	
4.3 Stress-Reduction Tactics for Pre-game Anxiety	
4.4 Building Confidence Through Positive Self-Talk	
4.5 Overcoming Fear of Failure On and Off the Field	
5. The Mind-Body Connection: Techniques to Enhance Both	49
5.1 Yoga and Pilates for Athletes: Strengthening the Mind-Body Link	

    5.2 The Role of Meditation in Athletic Recovery
    5.3 Integrating Mindfulness into Physical Training

6. Customized Fitness Routines Post-Covid   57
    6.1 Designing a 40-Minute High-Impact Workout for Teen Athletes
    6.2 Safety Guidelines: Injury Prevention and Recovery
    6.3 Adapting Training for Limited Access to Facilities
    6.4 Integrating Home Workouts for Strength and Flexibility
    6.5 The Importance of Rest and Active Recovery

7. Nutrition for Peak Performance   69
    7.1 Fueling Your Body: Nutrition Basics for Teen Athletes
    7.2 Hydration Strategies for Enhanced Performance
    7.3 Supplementation: What Works and What Doesn't
    7.4 Eating for Recovery: Post-workout Nutrition
    7.5 Managing Nutrition on Limited Budgets and Resources

8. Setting the Stage for Long-Term Athletic Success   79
    8.1 From High School to College Athletics: Planning Your Path
    8.2 The Role of Mentorship in Athletic Development
    8.3 Navigating Sponsorships and Media as a Young Athlete
    8.4 Anticipating and Adapting to Future Challenges in Sports

9. Beyond the Game: Life Skills from Sports   87
    9.1 Leadership and Teamwork: Lessons from the Field
    9.2 Time Management and Discipline: the Athlete's Advantage
    9.3 Resilience in Life: Applying Athletic Mental Toughness to Everyday Challenges

Conclusion   103
Dedication   109
References   111

Foreword

I met Tim Law around seven years ago. He contacted me after reading the first edition of my book, *Disconnected*. He told me that he was impressed with the work I was doing to help kids and families. Tim and I kept in contact, and as I got to know him, I came to realize what a special man he is. His life's calling is to turn boys into fine men and girls into fine women. Although Tim believes he does this through his many years of coaching and teaching, there's more to this process than meets the eye.

Having worked alongside countless teachers and coaches in my twenty-five-year career as a high school counselor, I've come across just a handful that truly had a gift, the "it factor." These individuals all shared one specific trait—they are born leaders. Tim is one of those leaders.

What exactly is a leader? Is a teacher a leader simply because they teach? Is a coach a leader simply because they coach? Is the captain of the tennis team or the class president a leader because they were chosen to be one? Not necessarily. Most leaders neither try to lead nor realize that they lead. It's something that is natural to them because it's based on how they live their own lives, which is deeply-rooted in character, passion, honesty, and integrity. And because of this, they have something called magnetism. People are drawn to them.

When Tim sent me the manuscript for this book and asked me to write the forward, I was honored and humbled. After scouring through the pages it became more obvious to me how much time and effort Tim puts into serving our nation's youth. The book covers every possible component of what it means to be a successful athlete, from nutrition to sleep to stretching, and most important of all, mental toughness. You see, Tim's tips, techniques, and strategies—while designed to help young folks excel in their sport—go much further than that; they help young folks become great adults and future leaders themselves.

When Tim speaks, everyone should listen.

— Tom Kersting, psychotherapist, author of
Disconnected and Raising Healthy Teenagers, speaker

★★★

"Fatigue makes cowards of us all." -Vince Lombardi,
Green Bay Packers' Legendary Coach

Our lives are a conveyor belt of daily challenges, some days more so than others. How crucially important is it to adapt our lives to this reality as we use these challenges to grow our mental toughness? This book will show you a stair-step, day-by-day method to growing your ability to successfully navigate the *real world*, not the idealized version that is falsely painted as reality.

One of the very best quotes I heard many years ago was from a mentor of mine by the name of Brian Tracy. He said, "Never wish for things to be easier; always work to make yourself stronger." Doing so with mental toughness will help you to find a wonderful quality of life. Here are a few other inspirational quotes that you can come back to whenever you need inspiration for the challenge:

"Success is a journey, not a destination.
The doing is often more important than the outcome."
-Arthur Ashe, tennis champion

> "Intelligence is the ability to make better distinctions."
> –Robert Kiyosaki, author of *Rich Dad, Poor Dad*

> "Make your life an example for others, not a warning."
> –Jim Rohn, self-help author

Throughout this read there will be examples of a variety of student athletes and others that have shared their stories of mental toughness. I define mental toughness as self-discipline, persistence, a healthy work ethic, self-reliance, long-term thinking (*not* instant gratification), and additional efforts that may take us out of the cocoon of our comfort zones. The importance of pushing through those comfort zones can't be overstated and is 100 percent necessary to grow into a self-reliant, self-motivated adult.

Unfortunately, our softening society has, in too many cases, created just the opposite, and we see examples of this sad scenario all around us every day. We all need to live in reality, not in some form of a fantasy.

As you develop mental toughness, you are also extending your quit point beyond others you may be competing with in a variety of arenas, whether on the fields of sports, in your career, or other areas of challenge. This is why developing the habit of going the extra mile in all you do will catapult you beyond most others you are coming up against. For those out there that have a "want to" and the courage to get off their backsides to gain more for their lives, this book will provide easy strategies to begin the process, regardless of where you may be currently in your efforts. There are many examples here of how you can fire up your own positive self-motivation so that you can enjoy more happiness and success in your life. Many of these strategies and techniques have already helped countless numbers of people.

Always remember this: YOU ARE WORTH IT! To quote the traditional saying, "Go for it!"

Introduction

The world as we knew it took an *unexpected turn* with the onset of the COVID-19 pandemic. For teen athletes like you, the impact was immediate and profound. Seasons were cut short, training moved online, and the camaraderie of team sports was replaced by isolation. The physical demands of sport did not vanish, but the mental and emotional toll intensified, presenting challenges that many were unprepared to handle.

This book emerges from a deep-seated passion for aiding young athletes like yourself to navigate and triumph over these new hurdles. With a background in sports psychology and coaching, I have witnessed firsthand the resilience and potential in each athlete to *rise above adversity*.

This guide is your roadmap to reclaiming your peak physical and mental fitness in a world that continues to grapple with the aftermath of a global crisis.

In the pages that follow, we'll explore the altered sports landscape, laying a foundation to understand the unique challenges and opportunities it presents. We will dive into strategies for *building* resilience, *enhancing* mental toughness, and *optimizing* your physical health. What sets this book apart is its focus on the specific nuances of the post-COVID recovery phase, backed by the latest research and packed with practical, actionable strategies tailored for teen athletes. You'll find compelling data underscoring the importance of mental and physical well-being, such as the significant drop in youth sports participation during the pandemic and the spike in mental health issues among athletes like you.

To inspire you further, I've included quotes from renowned figures in sports and real-life success stories of young athletes who have successfully adapted to the new norms. Their experiences are a testament to what can be achieved with determination and the right guidance.

Consider this book not just for reading but as a call to action. It's an invitation to step up, apply what you learn, and not just return to your former self but exceed what you thought was possible. Embrace this as your moment to transform challenges into stepping stones for growth and excellence.

As we embark on this journey together, remember that the path to greatness is often paved with obstacles. Yet, it is how you face these obstacles that defines your future. Let's begin this journey with *resilience* and *optimism*, ready to tackle what lies ahead with confidence and vigor.

Chapter 1

The New Normal for Teen Athletes

The Pull of Inertia

It is important to understand Newton's laws, using them to propel your life toward mental, physical, and emotional success.

Newton's first law states that every object will remain at rest or in uniform motion in a straight line unless compelled to change its state by the action of an external force. This tendency to resist changes in a state of motion is inertia. Doesn't this sound just like a couch potato?

A truism coined by Tony Robbins and used by many other thought-leaders states that the number one key to success is *personal power*. This is the ability (and willingness) to take action in our lives physically, mentally, and emotionally. Don't wait and expect anyone else to be concerned for you long term. Resist falling into the inertia described in Newton's first law. Make personal power a big part of your own why and let its principles form your self-reliance habits!

So, why am I addressing you as a teen athlete rather than your caregivers? Teens and children who endured everything that went with the pandemic had a much higher percentage of their lives impacted than an adult. For example, a fifteen-year-old would have had 2/15th's of their life disrupted versus a forty-year-old who had 2/40th's or 1/20th of their life impacted. Can you see that the younger the person experiencing the COVID-19 lockdowns the stronger the impact on them?

One such impact was the vastly increased use of electronic devices. The companies that run the various online platforms that appear on such devices use a lot of bells and whistles to grab the time and attention of their viewers. Not only that, but an untold number of hours of research have been spent on these platforms to see what the companies can do to *keep* viewers' focus on them. Unless there is a disciplined parent or guardian encouraging their child or teen to get off these devices, to get outside and move, the full impact of Newton's law of inertia comes into play!

Do you need proof? As you look around, you can see more and more people of all ages with their heads down for untold hours. Their eyes and minds are fully given over to their devices, along with their time and attention.

The evidence is *overwhelming*; the largest addiction in the world today is not drugs and alcohol but *screen addiction*, especially in their use as "entertainment."

Using these as a babysitter has become a very expensive long-term issue for millions of young people. Research has shown that if a young child is on these, the plasticity of their brain is changing, and not in a good way! Think of a child of ten years old or younger spending hours on screens being entertained rather than receiving a solid education filled with self-discipline. Their brains are being changed in ways that haven't been seen in eons of human development.

(For more excellent information on this issue, please check out my good friend and clinical psychologist Tom Kersting and his unparalleled research on the addictions of overuse of screen time. Raising Healthy Teenagers and Disconnected are both must reads to fully grasp the challenging overuse of screen time.)

Always remember, we are all free to make choices in our lives, but we are not free of the consequences (good or bad) of those choices. Being addicted to non-productive screen time will 100 percent lead to a very poor quality of life and future due to the negative habits that they create. This is 180 degrees away from the top key habit of personal power, which is taking action in our lives. Anything that interferes with the positive habit of actions—whether physically, mentally, or emotionally—is a direction we will regret.

Mental Toughness and Your Future

There are many faces to mental toughness, and within my YouTube channel, Playing It Forward Coaching, you can see several hundred interviews of those who are exhibiting mental toughness through the amazing things they are doing. (This channel was started during the COVID-19 lockdowns and, trust me when I say that, as a baby boomer, these interviews motivated me just as much as I hope they will motivate you. I truly had to pick up a number of skills not easily learned by people of my generation. It certainly forced me to use and apply mental toughness in many new ways as I learned several more skill sets.)

They include, but are not limited to, a woman who donated a kidney; a lady who received a heart transplant; an All-American female gymnast who tied the NCAA record with twenty-eight perfect-ten scores; and a former tennis player of mine who worked and prepared for ten years with the goal of scaling Mount Everest and did so!

Celebrating those who have successfully pushed through the cocoon of their comfort zones certainly provides inspiration for all of us to take actions in our own lives!

The great Ben Franklin, one of the most prodigious thought leaders of his time, said this regarding quality, productive days: "Plow deep while sluggards sleep and you shall have corn to sell and keep." Wise words then and just as wise now. Getting up and active early in the day takes a level of mental toughness and self-discipline that, for all of us willing to apply those skills, will definitely pay off in the long run.

A good friend of mine at Northeastern High School (and there are many amazing teachers there) Mr. Ben Weaver says to his classes daily, "Carpe Diem," or "seize the day." (Ironically and metaphorically, it means to "pluck the day," as it began as a horticultural term in Latin.)

Mr. Weaver successfully uses this to encourage and spur on his students to always do their best in his classes every day, and he succeeds incredibly well. Ben has had students too numerous to mention that have come back from college thanking him for helping them prepare for the rigors of college-level academia. This is another great example of mental toughness.

So, although this book is specifically looking at mental toughness for teen athletes post-COVID-19, a lot of the traits are tied in with the life skills we all need, making them relevant for now and transferrable to our futures. These include self-reliance; avoiding seeing ourselves as a victim; strategically developing a marketable skill set in higher education, such as attending a trade school or going into the military; the habit of a solid work ethic; developing a pleasing personality with our people skills; and going the extra mile for ourselves and others with additional positive action-oriented habits.

You will face challenges in life, and having a solid grasp on mental toughness will be to your advantage in any of the following situations:

- Having to change a tire in what may not be the best conditions on the road or in inclement weather.

- Your newborn baby needs you in the middle of the night. Your bed feels so comfortable but you do what has to be done in that moment for your child.

- Understanding life's ebb and flow with the births and deaths we will all experience from time to time.

- Taking the time to mentor a young person whose current personality is less than positive to deal with.

- The ability to handle the small frustrations we all face daily with grace and dignity without losing our cool. Humor can certainly be our ally in dealing with these.

- Staying patient with others when it appears they deserve less than that. For example, on the road with other drivers. An impatient honk on your horn could lead to consequences you and your family might regret!

- Understanding and applying karma in our lives and the importance of practicing the Golden Rule: "Treat others how you want to be treated."

- Packing to go on an anticipated vacation, which always seems to go by too fast, then taking the trip home and unpacking, all while doing so with a sense of gratitude for an enjoyable trip.

- Other unexpected challenges we all know that could visit us as a surprise we did not realize was coming.

The goal should be to follow the idea of a previous thought leader Henry-Louis Bergson (1859-1941), who coined the following phrase: "Think like a man (person) of action and act like a man (person) of thought."

By following this advice, you will not believe the increased quality of life you will achieve! In my time as a coach and teacher, I have observed that there are two main ways we feel good about ourselves: in our personal accomplishments and in our interpersonal relationships. Once we have these going for us, they put us in a position to overcome the negative parts of human nature, which is our tendency to trend toward that of selfishness and laziness—the opposites of mental toughness.

The employment of mental toughness also encourages each of us to be a better team player, not just with the people on our team but also with our families, friends, teachers, and other people we interact with around us. It takes the "me first" attitude and aligns it with the team or group we are working with.

Spend time developing mental toughness and the self-discipline to get your forty minutes of movement every day so that you can enhance your health, energy, and fitness to do more and be more. Forty minutes is only 1/36 of a twenty-four-hour day. These minutes can also be broken down into increments of five minutes here, fifteen minutes there, and twenty minutes later on. Doing just forty minutes a day works out to 1,200 minutes monthly and 14,400 minutes a year!

Review the time spent on your screens and devices for entertainment and vow to do a "digital diet," replacing at least some of that time with physical movement, reading a self-help book, or listening to ideas and music that further inspire us to do and become more in our life. Exercise self-discipline and mental toughness by keeping your screens and devices out of your bedroom for quality sleep every night.

Since the goal is a higher-quality life, incorporating small, daily mental toughness habits will transform your life in twenty-one to thirty days if applied with consistent quality, or CQ as I refer to it. We will expand on many of the following mentally tough health habits as the book continues because by applying them, I can literally assure you that you will feel your best everyday.

- Aim for proper sleep patterns every day, as this is the key habit many of us, not just teens, violate. Getting an inappropriate amount of sleep makes our days drag on, leaving us feeling too tired to get through the things that need doing.

- Get the right combination of nutrition and hydration to keep yourself healthy and energetic. You will accomplish more every day for yourself and others.

- Engage in consistent quality (CQ) exercise that matches your daily demands.

- Dress properly for the weather conditions, as they definitely can vary depending on where you live.

- Maintain a positive mental attitude, which is arguably the most important health habit, as this will kick off happy hormones known as endorphins, which will further enhance your outlook on life.

- Develop the habit of positive self-talk, as it can and will carry you through the challenging times we all face. By doing this, you blow up your own internal self-image balloon. In a world of seemingly non-stop negativity from a variety of sources, including social media, managing your own mental state has never been more important. Avoid the negative issues that surround all of us and focus your attention on gratitude for the things, opportunities, and good people around you.

It's worth mentioning again here that we are all free to make choices in our lives, but we are not free of the consequences (good or bad) of the choices we do make. Thank you for your choice of reading this far into the book!

The Power of Manners

Speaking of consequences, good or bad, one of the very best ways for you as a young person to create value for yourself and accelerate your position in the world is by developing good manners at an early age. Think of it this way, as a young person, your world experience is certainly not that deep, nor is it expected to be. By developing good manners, you will be on the fast track to success, as the adults around you will look to bring you more opportunities.

I can't begin to tell you how many young people I have endorsed or written letters of recommendation for and, sadly, many of whom I did not due to surly, disrespectful attitudes toward others.

As always, I will do my best to include key resources that will assist you in receiving a positive consequence for those willing to take the steps. One of the amazing timeless classics on good manners and people skills is Dale Carnegie's book, *How to Win Friends and Influence People*.

Capturing the skills included in this great read is like capturing the knowledge that oil and not sand goes into a car engine. Sand will destroy the engine, just like bad manners will destroy relationships between yourself and others. Oil, on the other hand, will lubricate the engine, just as good manners lubricates relations between you and those around you. The number of times I have had the chance to de-escalate a potential classroom or public altercation with this skill set are too many to list but they work!

Read on for more very doable skills (a.k.a., habits) that will add quality to the lives of those practicing them. Always remember, just one new, good idea can help any of us improve our lives, and this book has some of the best I have ever discovered.

What Gets Measured, Gets Managed

Keep track daily of the amount of non-productive time you spend on these addiction machines and always move forward on a "digital diet." Using these for solid productivity is a good choice; using them for non-stop entertainment is a recipe for future disaster! Take charge of your time, energy, and attention and stop conceding them to the tech giants to have it squandered. Their goal is to grab as much of your time and attention as possible!

Speaking of what gets measured, gets managed, is the importance of using positive affirmations while continuing to workout and visualize. The one I use consistently while doing dips, pull-ups, push-ups, etc is counting, "GRIT 1, GRIT 2, GRIT 3 and so on. Using the G.R.I.T. acronym with this self-talk affirmation meaning of Greater Results/ Intense Training pushes me to do a little more until hitting failure with a particular workout.

Regarding my particular exercises, I believe it is important to emphasize key areas with our push muscles, such as push ups, dips; pull muscles as with pull ups/chin ups; squats with a weight you can comfortably handle and finally; abdominal with leg raises, crunches and other variations. I believe these four areas of our body represent the main parts we should be keeping in shape and toned.

Another important variable to do a few times a week has to do with our balance and can be easily accomplished by standing on one leg for 20-25 seconds and then the other leg. Small disciplines such as these can definitely lead to better balance and less chances of a fall. Balance is important! Please don't ignore it.

It doesn't have to be a long exercise, but helps your intensity and pushes out your "quit point." Being able to use this skill will pay dividends throughout your life when you need to "pop the accelerator" and have the energy to get an important task completed on time with Consistent Quality, "CQ!"

1.1 Navigating the Shift: Sports in a Post-Covid World

As a teen athlete, you've likely felt the ground shift beneath your feet over the past few years. The familiar rhythms of practice, competition, and teamwork were disrupted almost overnight, replaced by a landscape where uncertainty seemed to be the only certainty. This new normal isn't just a phase; it's a reshaped arena that demands adaptability, resilience, and an innovative spirit from athletes like you.

Whether it was swapping the track, court, or field for the living room or backyard, or meeting teammates and coaches on screens instead of in person, the way you train, compete, and connect has transformed. The rest of this chapter is about understanding these shifts, embracing the changes, and finding ways to turn challenges into opportunities for growth and excellence in your athletic pursuits.

In fact, I believe that recapturing our personal power after experiencing the pandemic is so important that I will spend the first half of this book taking you through the multitude of ways that teen athletes like you were affected by the changes and restrictions on sports during the pandemic. It's important that we see how these changes actually gave us powerful "whys" and how they can help us move from the inertia encouraged during the pandemic to walking in more of our personal power.

Remember this important point as you continue to read: nobody can motivate you but you. I can offer you positive self-motivation skills and tools for success, but it's your job to pick up those tools, make the choice to get active, and walk forward with purpose.

Shift in Training Modalities

The closure of training facilities was more than just a logistical inconvenience; it was a call to rethink and reshape the very way athletes prepare themselves. Without access to the usual training grounds, a significant pivot toward individualized and home-based training programs emerged. This shift wasn't just about maintaining physical condition but also about developing self-motivation and discipline in environments that were not traditionally associated with high-intensity training. Flexibility became all important. You may have seen your coach turn living rooms, garages, and backyards into makeshift gyms, leveraging everything from household items to specialized apps to guide and track progress. This adaptation not only kept athletes in shape but also ingrained a level of *self-reliance* that has the potential to *redefine* training regimes even beyond the pandemic.

Adaptation to Virtual Competitions

We talked previously about the dangers of inertia while spending too much time being entertained by a screen. COVID-19 also presented athletes with an opportunity to use screens to aid their mental toughness. This was because the concept of competition took on a new form. Virtual meets and competitions became the norm, challenging athletes to stay competitive and motivated without the immediate physical presence of their competitors or the adrenaline rush of a live audience. This scenario required a mental shift into understanding that the competitive edge had to be internally driven. The essence of competition had to be distilled into its purest form: competing against yourself, striving to beat personal bests, and pushing limits from the isolation of your training space. The psychological resilience built during this time was invaluable, and even has the potential to transform how you approach competitions in the future.

Regulatory Changes in Sports

As the world opened back up, it cautiously stepped back into more active engagement bound by new rules and regulations, which needed to be navigated as often as they were updated. Sports, too, became bound by new rules and regulations designed to safeguard the health of participants. These ranged from reduced capacities at venues to strict protocols around physical contact. Navigating these rules required flexibility and patience from you as the landscape continued to evolve.

Opportunities for Innovation

Every challenge presents a hidden opportunity, and this shift was no exception. The constraints imposed by the pandemic sparked a wave of innovation within sports training and development. Coaches began to employ technology not just for training purposes but also for strategy sessions and mental health support, ensuring that athletes remained sharp and engaged. New training methodologies that required minimal equipment and space were developed during this time and are still becoming more refined. This stands to benefit those individuals who previously faced barriers to entry.

So you can see that this new era we've stepped into is about more than just getting back to the way things were. It's about moving forward with new tools, insights, and a renewed appreciation for the role sports play in fostering resilience, community, and health. As you navigate this new landscape, remember that the qualities that define great athletes—adaptability, resilience, and a relentless pursuit of excellence—remain your most valuable assets.

1.2 FROM ISOLATION TO INTEGRATION: REBUILDING TEAM DYNAMICS

The sudden shift to a more isolated lifestyle during the pandemic posed significant challenges, not just physically but psychologically, particularly for athletes who were accustomed to the highly social environment of team sports. The absence of daily interactions, group practices, and the communal striving toward common goals led many young people to feelings of disconnection and loneliness, impacting mental health and overall well-being. The disruption of these dynamics also had the potential to weaken team cohesion, a foundational component of any collective athletic endeavor.

Understanding the psychological impacts of this isolation is crucial. It has been observed that prolonged disconnection can lead to a decrease in motivation and a sense of alienation among teammates, which in turn affects performance both on and off the field. As athletes, part of your identity is tied to your role within the team, and having spent time removed from this setting, you may still be left with feelings of a loss in your identity.

Addressing these challenges requires *intentional strategies* focused on rebuilding the fabric of team unity and solidarity. Coaches and team leaders play a pivotal role here, as they can create opportunities for connections that bridge the physical gap. Organizing team-building activities helps strengthen weakened bonds. However, these teams also need you. Being willing to interact again and bring your full personal power to your team helps to preserve the heart and soul of the team.

In the thick of physical distancing, screen use surged to the forefront, being seen as an essential element in maintaining team spirit. Platforms that allow video calls, real-time messaging, and shared digital spaces became the arenas where team dynamics evolved. These tools were used creatively not just for training purposes but for maintaining a team's emotional and psychological pillars. Now that teams are no longer required to remain socially distanced and online isn't the only place they can connect, technology can go back to an appropriate minimal level of use. For example, YouTube videos of great athletes and sports performances can be watched to help with your visualization efforts. The challenge comes when these platforms are being used primarily for entertainment that wastes time rather than providing useful resources. To quote self-help expert Brian Tracy, "Entertainment should be life's desserts, not the main course."

Two big parts of mental toughness are applying self-discipline consistently to our lives and thinking long term. They are both important in the formula for long-term success and happiness, allowing us to accomplish many valuable goals.

1.3 The Psychological Impact of Missing Key Competitions

The cancellation or postponement of key competitions was much more than a mere schedule adjustment; it often felt like a significant personal loss. For many athletes, competitions are not just about the sport itself but are deeply intertwined with personal identity and life rhythm. They offer a sense of *purpose* and a structured *goal* to work toward. When these events were suddenly stripped from your calendar, it's understandable if the disappointment was profound, even perhaps triggering a crisis of identity. You might have found yourself questioning your role as an athlete when you weren't able to compete, or have felt a void where your passion and drive used to reside. It's easy to forget these feelings now that we're post-pandemic, but it's also normal if you have thoughts like, "What if something similar happens again?"

First, understanding this emotional toll is crucial. It's normal to have felt a range of emotions—from frustration and sadness to anger and confusion—when competitions were canceled. These feelings were valid responses to your disrupted plans and dreams. However, dwelling on what might have been is a pathway to deeper discontent. Instead, this is an opportunity to build mental toughness, a skill as critical as any physical capability you train for. Mental toughness, or mental resilience, isn't about not feeling disappointment—it's about finding ways to *move forward despite it*.

One effective strategy is to actively maintain a positive outlook. This can be challenging, especially in the face of uncertainty, but focusing on elements within your control can be empowering. For instance, while you can't control event schedules, you can control your training routines, mindset, and how you respond to these disruptions. Engage in mental training exercises such as visualization and positive self-talk. Visualize yourself overcoming current challenges and achieving future goals, and replace negative thoughts with affirmations about your strength and capability. Remember, mental toughness is like a muscle—the more you work it, the stronger it becomes.

Setting new, achievable goals can be another step if previous goals are suddenly unattainable due to circumstances outside your control. Goals that are within reach and that keep you motivated help to redirect your focus. These might be related to improving specific skills, increasing your physical conditioning, or even personal growth objectives like enhancing your leadership qualities or learning a new aspect of your sport. Decide exactly what you want; get excited about it by setting your goal to a high but achievable standard; write it down every day and read it morning and night. For example, if you're a swimmer and can't compete, you might set a goal to perfect your butterfly stroke technique or improve your start and turn times.

By doing this, you activate the part of your brain known as the Reticular Activating System. An everyday example of this is when you are looking at making a large purchase; for example, a car. You're researching a particular model of a vehicle and suddenly you start seeing the same model as you're out driving, running errands, in parking lots, etc. Those vehicles were always out there, but they went unnoticed by you until you started spending mental energy on researching them.

Firing up the Reticular Activating System by setting goals helps you notice keys that, in turn, help you take the steps needed to reach your goals. It enables you to pull events, circumstances, and people into your life that will allow you to accelerate your progress.

Lastly, never underestimate the importance of a *robust* support system. The path of an athlete is rarely walked alone, and this is especially true in times of crisis. Lean on your coaches, family, and peers. Your coaches can provide modified training plans and techniques to keep you progressing, while family and friends offer emotional support, ensuring you feel understood and valued beyond your athletic performance. Staying connected through regular check-ins, can help you to express your feelings and concerns. Sometimes, simply sharing your experiences can lighten your emotional load and provide new perspectives that *reframe* your situation.

Navigating the emotional landscape of missing competitions requires a multifaceted approach where mental resilience, goal redefinition, and community support are interwoven. But remember that if you have to adapt to sudden changes again, those challenges also hold an opportunity for growth. The skills and strength you developed during the pandemic will be invaluable assets, helping you emerge as a more resilient and versatile athlete ready to embrace any future challenges.

Chapter 2

Mental Health and Wellness Post-Covid

In the whirlwind that followed the onset of the Covid-19 pandemic, the world shifted in ways both obvious and subtle, impacting everything from global economies to personal daily routines. For you, as a teen athlete, these changes transcended the physical realms of training and competition, seeping into the mental and emotional fabrics of your life. This chapter aims to address a crucial aspect often shadowed by physical fitness: mental health and wellness in the post-Covid era. Here, you'll discover not just the challenges but also the strategies and supports that can guide you through these uncharted waters, helping you to not only recover but thrive.

It has been stated by Tony Robbins that "motion creates emotion." I truly believe that people who have developed the habit of consistent movement are not only more fit physically but also mentally and emotionally. As we move along the fitness pathway we can't help impacting two main ways we feel good about ourselves: our personal accomplishments and getting along well with other people. These happen as we develop skill sets that create value for others and the world.

If we are missing either of these two, our lives are not as fulfilling as they could be. Always remember, we are free to make choices in our lives but are not free of the consequences of those choices.

2.1 Recognizing Post-COVID-19 Anxiety and Its Effects on Performance

Symptoms and Signs

Post-COVID-19 anxiety in athletes like yourself can manifest in several ways, some subtle and others more overt. You might find yourself experiencing persistent worries about future competitions, fear of injury, or concerns about contracting or transmitting the virus. Physically, anxiety might present as increased heart rate, rapid breathing, or an inability to relax, even off the field. It's also common to feel irritability, difficulty concentrating, or a sense of being overwhelmed, which can make routine training feel more daunting. Recognizing these signs is the first step toward managing them effectively.

Impact on Athletic Performance

Anxiety isn't just a battle of the mind; it has tangible effects on your performance as well. High levels of stress and anxiety can lead to muscle tension, coordination problems, and fatigue, which all affect how well you perform. Mentally, it can cloud your decision-making, reduce your focus, and diminish your confidence, all of which are crucial for peak performance in sports. The mental chatter and worry that accompany anxiety consume significant mental energy—energy that could otherwise be directed towards your training and performance.

Coping Mechanisms

Managing anxiety involves a combination of mindfulness techniques, structured relaxation, and practical anxiety-reduction strategies. Mindfulness can anchor you in the present moment and reduce the tendency to ruminate on "what ifs." Techniques such as focused breathing, meditation, or yoga can significantly lower stress levels, making them powerful tools in your mental health toolkit. For instance, practicing diaphragmatic breathing before a game or training session can help calm your mind and body, setting a more focused tone for your athletic engagement.

Structured relaxation techniques, such as progressive muscle relaxation or guided imagery, can also play a crucial role. These methods not only ease the physical symptoms of anxiety but also prepare your mind for the challenges ahead, allowing you to approach your training with a calmer, more centered mindset. Implementing these techniques regularly can help mitigate the intensity of anxiety symptoms over time, making them less likely to interfere with your sports performance.

Professional Support

While self-help strategies are effective, there are times when professional support is needed. If anxiety is significantly impacting your life and performance, seeking help from a mental health professional can provide relief and introduce new coping strategies tailored to your specific needs. Sports psychologists, in particular, are trained to address the mental challenges associated with athletic performance, including anxiety management.

Finding the right professional may seem daunting, but you can start by consulting with your coach or athletic director who likely has connections to sports psychologists who specialize in working with young athletes. Additionally, telehealth services have made it easier to access mental health resources, allowing you to receive support from the comfort of your home. Engaging with a professional is not a sign of weakness but a proactive step towards strengthening your mental fortitude and enhancing your athletic performance.

In managing post-Covid anxiety, remember that it's not about eradicating anxiety completely but learning to control and navigate it so that it doesn't control you. By recognizing the signs, understanding the impact, employing coping strategies, and seeking help when necessary, you empower yourself not just to cope with anxiety but to rise above it, reclaiming your mental space and focus for peak performance. As you integrate these practices into your life, they'll not only improve your athletic performance but also enhance your overall well-being, teaching you skills that are valuable both on and off the field.

2.2 Strategies for Managing Depression

Depression among teen athletes is a significant concern, especially in the post-COVID-19 era where the usual stressors of competitive sports combine with the isolation and disruptions you experienced during the pandemic. It's vital to understand that feeling down occasionally is a part of life, but depression is more than just temporary sadness. It can manifest as a persistent feeling of emptiness, a lack of energy, or a disinterest in activities that once brought joy. It can significantly impact daily functioning and athletic performance. Recognizing the prevalence of depression is the first step. You are not alone; depression affects a considerable number of young athletes. Physical activity is widely recognized for its positive effects on mental health, acting as a natural antidepressant. It stimulates the release of endorphins, known as "feel-good" hormones, which can improve mood and reduce feelings of depression. Maintaining a regular exercise regimen can provide structure and a sense of normalcy, and the physical improvements and achievements can boost self-esteem and counter feelings of helplessness or hopelessness often associated with depression.

Seeking professional help is a critical step for any athlete struggling with depression. It's important to recognize when symptoms have escalated beyond the normal scope of sadness and are affecting daily life and performance. Therapy, particularly cognitive-behavioral therapy (CBT), has been shown to be effective in treating depression. CBT helps individuals manage their depression by changing negative patterns of thought and behavior into more positive ones. Additionally, in some cases, medication may be prescribed alongside therapy to help alleviate the symptoms of depression. Finding the right therapist or counselor, someone you can trust and feel comfortable speaking with, is essential. Many resources are available, from school counselors and sports psychologists to mental health professionals specializing in adolescent therapy.

As you continue to engage with your sport, remember that taking care of your mental health is just as important as honing your physical skills, and seeking help is a sign of strength, not weakness.

2.3 The Role of Sleep in Mental and Physical Recovery

Sleep is often the unsung hero in the arsenal of tools available to athletes for optimal performance and recovery. It's during those crucial hours of rest that your body undergoes repair and your mind consolidates memories and processes emotions, which are essential for both physical and mental health. For athletes like you, sleep isn;t just a break from the day;s activities; i;'s a critical period for enhancing everything from muscle recovery to strategic thinking and emotional resilience. Without adequate sleep, your body can't repair itself effectively, and your mental sharpness and mood can suffer, which in turn can impact your performance in both training and competitions.

Back in my time of being a teen athlete, getting quality sleep, along with excellent nutrition, hydration, and visualization weren't habits separate from training; they *were* training. However, maintaining good sleep hygiene has become more challenging in the post-COVID-19 era. Increased screen time during the pandemic, due to both online schooling and social interactions shifting to digital platforms, likely disrupted your natural sleep patterns. The blue light emitted by screens can interfere with the production of melatonin, the hormone that regulates sleep-wake cycles, making it harder to fall asleep and stay asleep. Additionally, the stress and uncertainty brought about by the pandemic may have led to increased anxiety, which is another significant barrier to restful sleep. These challenges are notable not just for their immediate effects but for their potential to set patterns that might disrupt your sleep long-term.

A quote by Lord Jonathan Sacks sums this up perfectly: "The single most important distinction in life is to distinguish between an opportunity to be seized and temptation to be resisted." I'll leave it up to you to figure out which category most screen time falls into.

To counter these challenges and enhance your sleep quality, establishing a solid nighttime routine is crucial. Start by setting a consistent bedtime and wake-up time that allows for seven to nine hours of sleep, which is the recommended amount for teenagers. This consistency helps regulate your body's internal clock and can improve the quality of your sleep. Make your pre-sleep routine calming and free from intense physical or mental activities. Engaging in relaxing activities such as reading a book, listening to soothing music, or practicing relaxation exercises can signal to your body that it's time to wind down.

Try to make your bedroom a sleep-inducing environment. Keep it cool, quiet, and dark, and invest in a comfortable mattress and pillows. Consider using blackout curtains or an eye mask to block out light, and perhaps some white noise or gentle background sounds to drown out disruptive noises.

Most importantly, limit exposure to screens at least an hour before bedtime. If you cannot avoid using your devices, consider adjusting the screen settings to reduce blue light exposure or use glasses that block blue light. Incorporating these strategies into your daily routine can significantly enhance your ability to get restful sleep, which is indispensable for your recovery and performance as an athlete. Remember, sleep is as crucial to your athletic success as your training regimen. By prioritizing and improving your sleep routine, you're not only investing in better performance but also in a healthier, more resilient you.

2.4 Nutrition for the Mind: Eating for Mental Toughness

The connection between what you eat and how you feel is profound, yet it's often overlooked in the athletic world where the focus tends to lean heavily on physical performance. However, as a young athlete, it's crucial to understand that your mental health is just as important as your physical health, and what you consume can play a significant role in maintaining a balanced emotional state. The brain, like any other part of the body, requires a variety of nutrients to function optimally. Studies suggest that diets high in refined sugars, for example, are harmful to the brain. They not only worsen mood but may also impair brain functions over time. Conversely, diets rich in vegetables, fruits, unprocessed grains, and fish, which provide an abundance of nutrients, can promote better brain health.

To dive deeper, certain foods have been directly linked to brain health and emotional well-being. Omega-3 fatty acids, for instance, found abundantly in fish like salmon and sardines, are essential for cognitive function and mental health. They play a crucial role in building brain and nerve cells, which are fundamental for learning and memory, not to mention their ability to fight off depression. Similarly, antioxidants in berries help combat inflammation and oxidative stress, factors that are linked to mood disorders and depression. Incorporating a variety of these nutrient-rich foods can help stabilize your mood, clear your mind, and enhance your overall emotional resilience and mental toughness.

When it comes to meal planning, the goal is to ensure that your diet supports both physical and mental health. Start by structuring meals around whole foods, focusing on a balance of carbohydrates, proteins, and fats to stabilize blood sugar levels and provide a steady source of energy throughout the day. Carbohydrates are particularly important for brain function, so choose complex carbohydrates like whole grains, fruits, and vegetables over simple sugars to prevent the highs and lows associated with sugar spikes.

Protein, like complex carbohydrates, helps to regulate your mood. Some foods rich in protein are lean meats, eggs, and legumes.

Hydration, too, plays a critical yet often underestimated role in mental health. Dehydration can lead to fatigue, irritability, and difficulty concentrating, all of which can negatively impact your mental state and athletic performance. The brain is approximately 75 percent water, and even mild dehydration can lead to a reduction in brain volume, affecting its function. Ensuring you drink enough water throughout the day is a simple yet effective way to stay hydrated. Aim to drink at least eight to ten glasses of water a day, more if you are active and sweat a lot during training. Remember, when you feel thirsty, your body is already moving toward dehydration. Keeping a water bottle handy during both training and throughout the day can help you maintain optimal levels.

Incorporating these dietary practices doesn't have to be a chore or a drastic departure from your current habits. It can be as simple as adding a serving of vegetables to each meal, swapping out sugary snacks for fruits or nuts, or choosing brown rice over white. Small, consistent changes can lead to significant improvements in both your physical and mental health, enhancing your ability to handle stress, regulate your mood, and maintain a high level of performance both on and off the field.

As you adjust your diet, pay attention to how these changes affect your mood and energy levels. This self-awareness can help you fine-tune your diet to best support your mental health needs, making you a more resilient and balanced athlete.

As we conclude this chapter, reflect on the diverse strategies discussed. Strategies that help you to find support for your mental and emotional health post-COVID-19 and help you look forward to how to grow even closer to reaching your future goals. This foundation of support is not just a safety net but a launching pad for your growth and success, both on the field and off.

As we transition into the next chapter, we will explore further how you can harness your mental and physical capacities to not only recover from setbacks but also to thrive in your future endeavors, equipped with a robust support system and an empowered mindset.

Chapter 3

Core Principles of Resilience for Athletes

Resilience is often pictured as the grit and grind to push through barriers, but for athletes like you, it means something deeper and more encompassing because it's a key pinnacle of mental toughness. Imagine resilience as a dynamic, multifaceted essence at the core of your being, one that ebbs and flows with life's varied challenges, transforming potential setbacks into opportunities for growth and learning. This chapter dives into what resilience truly means for an athlete, extending beyond mere perseverance to include adaptability, recovery, and personal growth. It's about bouncing back stronger, wiser, and more prepared than ever before.

3.1 Understanding Resilience: More than Just Grit

Broadening the Definition

Resilience is not just about enduring; it's also about adapting and thriving. Think of it as the capacity to recover quickly from difficulties, but also the ability to embrace change and use it as a stepping stone for growth. For you, as an athlete, this might mean adapting your training routines in response to an injury or a global pandemic, finding new ways to connect with your teammates despite physical distance, or adjusting your strategies based on a performance that didn't go as planned. When you are able to see setbacks as not just obstacles to overcome but as integral to the process of becoming a better athlete and a stronger individual, you are able to walk in more of your personal power.

Biopsychosocial Model of Resilience

Resilience is shaped by a combination of biological, psychological, and social factors. The biopsychosocial model provides a comprehensive framework that helps explain why some athletes bounce back faster or better than others. Biologically, your genetic makeup and physical health play a role. Psychologically, your personal coping mechanisms, emotional intelligence, and mindset determine how you handle stress and setbacks. Socially, the support systems you have in place, like your relationships with family, friends, coaches, and teammates, provide external resources that can bolster your internal strengths. Understanding how these all work together will help you identify which areas might need more attention or development to enhance your overall resilience.

Resilience in Sports Context

In sports, resilience can manifest in several key areas. Injury recovery is a primary aspect, where your ability to bounce back not just physically but mentally matters immensely. How quickly and effectively you can return to play after an injury often depends on your pre-injury preparation and post-injury care, both physically and mentally. This is why it's important to use your time wisely. Lessening the amount of hours spent on time-wasting activities on your devices and increasing time spent in training will benefit you in shortening your post-injury care.

Dealing with performance setbacks is another aspect of resilience that is crucial for athletes. Every athlete faces performances that don't meet their expectations, but resilient athletes use these experiences as fuel to improve, analyzing what went wrong and developing strategies to enhance future performances. This ability to learn from failure and keep moving forward is what sets resilient athletes apart.

Building Blocks of Resilience

Several key components construct an athlete's resilience. Optimism is one, where maintaining a positive outlook enables you to see beyond the immediate setbacks and keep focused on long-term goals.

Flexibility is another; being able to adapt your goals and methods in the face of new challenges is crucial. Mental toughness, characterized by persistence and tenacity, allows you to maintain your course even under pressure.

Together, these elements create a robust framework for resilience, supporting you in navigating the highs and lows of your athletic journey with grace and strength.

Visual Element: the Resilience Wheel

To better visualize the concept of resilience in sports, imagine a wheel where each spoke represents a different component of resilience—optimism, flexibility, mental toughness, physical health, emotional intelligence, and social support. The hub at the center of the wheel is you, integrating all these aspects to navigate your path in sports with resilience and determination. This wheel keeps rolling, adapting to the terrain, sometimes facing obstacles, at other times cruising smoothly, but always moving forward. This resilience wheel not only helps you understand the complexity of resilience but also serves as a reminder that each component is crucial and needs attention to keep the wheel balanced and functional.

As you continue to develop as an athlete, think of resilience not just as a trait to be admired but as a skill to be cultivated and nurtured. It's a dynamic, evolving capacity that can significantly determine how far you go in your sports career and how deeply you enjoy the journey. By understanding and integrating the principles of resilience discussed here, you equip yourself with the tools to face any challenge, transform setbacks into comebacks, and continue to grow, both on and off the field.

3.2 Setting and Adjusting Goals in Uncertain Times

In the ever-evolving landscape of athletics, especially amid the uncertainties brought about by global events like the COVID-19 pandemic, the ability to set flexible goals became crucial. Flexibility in goal-setting doesn't mean lowering your standards or losing sight of your ambitions; rather, it's about adapting your aims to accommodate and leverage new realities.

Imagine you're training for a national competition, and it gets postponed indefinitely. Instead of viewing this as a setback, you could shift your focus to improving individual skills or techniques, which can be just as rewarding and will likely enhance your performance when the competition is eventually rescheduled. This flexibility helps maintain your motivation and keeps you moving forward even when your original plans are disrupted. And when the opportunity arises again, you'll be ready to perform at your best.

Applying the SMART criteria—Specific, Measurable, Achievable, Relevant, Time-bound—to your sports goals can transform how you approach your athletic ambitions. For instance, if you're a swimmer aiming to improve your race times, a SMART goal might be to decrease your 100-meter freestyle time by two seconds within the next three months. This goal is specific (targeting a particular aspect of your performance), measurable (quantified by the time decrease), achievable (challenging yet within reach), relevant (directly impacts your competitive performance), and time-bound (set for a three-month period). By framing your goals in this way, you can create a clear roadmap for your training, making it easier to stay focused and measure your progress.

Adjusting your goals in the aftermath of setbacks like injuries or event cancellations is another key aspect of maintaining resilience in sports. When faced with an injury, for instance, your immediate goal might shift from performance-based to recovery-focused. This could mean setting goals around rehabilitation exercises or gradually increasing your training intensity based on guidance from medical and coaching professionals. This approach ensures that you are still progressing, albeit in a different direction, keeping your spirits up and your body in tune with the demands of your sport. Celebrating small wins along the way is essential for sustaining motivation and focus. Small victories, such as achieving a weekly training target or mastering a new technique, might seem minor in the grand scheme of your athletic career, but they play a significant role in building your confidence and sense of accomplishment. Each *small win* is a building block in the architecture of your larger ambitions, and acknowledging them can reinforce your commitment to your sport and your goals. Create a habit of recognizing these achievements; maybe keep a journal of daily or weekly successes, no matter how small. This will provide you with a tangible record of your progress, as well as boosting your morale and enthusiasm for the hard work ahead.

As you navigate through these uncertain times, remember that goal setting is not just about the endpoint but also about the journey. Each adjustment, each small win is a step forward in your development as an athlete and a person. Embrace the challenges and changes as opportunities to learn and grow, and use the SMART framework to keep your goals clear and focused. With flexibility, resilience, and a positive outlook, you can continue to advance toward your aspirations, regardless of the hurdles along the way.

3.3 Embracing Vulnerability as Strength

In the competitive realm of sports, where strength, speed, and stoicism are often prized above all, the concept of vulnerability can be assigned a lesser value. Traditionally, athletes are taught to mask their fears, hide their insecurities, and never show weakness. However, this mindset is shifting. More and more, vulnerability is being recognized as a profound strength, particularly when it comes to mental resilience and team dynamics. When you, as an athlete, embrace your vulnerabilities, you open up a pathway to genuine growth and deeper connections with your teammates and coaches.

Redefining vulnerability starts by understanding that it is a universal human condition. Like everyone else, you experience doubts, fears, and uncertainties. Acknowledging these feelings does not diminish your strength; rather, it enhances your ability to confront and manage them effectively. In sports, this might mean admitting that you're nervous about a big game, unsure about your recovery from an injury, or struggling to balance school and training. By embracing these vulnerabilities, you set the stage for personal growth. It allows you to tackle these issues head-on, seek the necessary resources or support, and grow from the experience. Moreover, recognizing your vulnerabilities can lead to improved self-awareness, which is crucial for personal development and peak performance.

There are a number of prominent athletes who have openly shared their struggles with mental health issues, the pressures of competition, or the challenges of coming back from injuries. Athletes such as Michael Phelps and Simone Biles have become powerful role models for embracing vulnerability. They show that vulnerability can coexist with tremendous strength and resilience. Their openness humanizes them while also breaking down the stigma around vulnerability, showing that it is possible to be both vulnerable and successful.

As you continue to navigate your athletic and personal development, consider how embracing vulnerability can enhance your performance and relationships. It's a tool that, when wielded with courage and confidence, can transform challenges into opportunities for growth. By redefining vulnerability in your own life and within your team, you contribute to a culture where resilience is built not just on physical prowess but on emotional and psychological support as well. This approach prepares you to handle the pressures of competitive sports, as well as equipping you with the emotional intelligence to succeed in all areas of life.

3.4 Cultivating a Growth Mindset Amidst Setbacks

The concepts of growth and fixed mindsets, as introduced by psychologist Carol Dweck, offer a profound understanding of how your beliefs about ability and potential can shape your sports experience and overall life. A fixed mindset holds the belief that skills and intelligence are static, leading you to avoid challenges that might expose your limits. Conversely, a growth mindset thrives on challenge and sees failure not as evidence of unintelligence but as a heartening springboard for growth and for stretching existing abilities. Within the athletic realm, this mindset dictates how you respond to setbacks, enhancing or hindering your development and performance.

Developing a growth mindset begins with recognizing that every challenge is an opportunity to learn. Think of this as pushing out beyond your comfort zone or quit point. You can use the acronym G.R.I.T.—Greater Results/Intense Training—to remind yourself to push to a higher level of effort.

Instead of shying away from tasks that might seem daunting, see them as opportunities to expand your skills. For instance, if a new technique in your sport feels difficult, instead of thinking, "I can't do this," try adopting a perspective like, "I can't do this YET but with practice, I'll get better." This subtle shift in thinking can significantly alter your approach to training and competition, infusing your practice sessions with a sense of purpose and excitement, no matter the difficulty of the tasks at hand.

Feedback, both positive and negative, is another crucial element in fostering a growth mindset. Constructive criticism isn't just necessary; it's a valuable tool for improvement. The key is to listen actively and see feedback as a gift that helps you understand your areas of improvement. For instance, if your coach points out a flaw in your technique, instead of taking it personally, use it as a cue to focus your practice and make adjustments. Over time, this receptivity to feedback can transform your performance, turning perceived weaknesses into areas of strength and mastery.

Applying a growth mindset to your training and competition involves embracing every outcome as a learning opportunity. Whether you win or lose, focus on what the experience taught you. Did you discover a weakness in your strategy that you can improve? Or perhaps you identified a strength that you hadn't fully appreciated before? For example, after a less successful game or match, instead of brooding over the loss, evaluate your performance to identify what went well and what didn't. This analysis will not only prepare you better for future competitions but also build resilience, adaptability, and mental toughness, qualities that define successful athletes.

In the long run, a growth mindset will enhance your satisfaction in your sport. When you focus on growth and learning, the intrinsic joy of improving and mastering new skills can be as rewarding as winning. This satisfaction can sustain your motivation over the long term, fueling your commitment to your sport and your personal development.

As you continue to cultivate a growth mindset, remember that setbacks and challenges are natural components of any athletic career. They are not markers of defeat but opportunities for growth and learning. Embrace these experiences, learn from them, and allow them to propel you forward in your athletic journey. This mindset is not a trait that some athletes are born with and others are not; it's a *skill* that can be developed and refined over time with practice and persistence. By choosing to adopt a growth mindset, you are setting yourself on a path of continuous improvement, resilience, and ultimately, greater achievement in sports and beyond.

The principles we have discussed in this chapter are more than just strategies; they are transformative approaches that can profoundly impact your performance, mindset, and enjoyment of sports. By understanding the power of resilience, the importance of goal flexibility, a growth mindset, and the strength found in vulnerability, you equip yourself with the tools to not only face challenges but to thrive in the face of them. As we move forward, carry these insights with you, applying them to both your athletic endeavors and your personal growth. What lies ahead is an exciting journey of learning and development, one that promises to be as rewarding as it is challenging.

Chapter 4

Practical Strategies for Enhanced Mental Toughness

In this journey of athletic excellence, mental toughness stands out as a beacon guiding you through challenges, setbacks, and triumphs. While physical prowess is visible and often celebrated, the quiet resilience of the mind is your unsung hero. This chapter is dedicated to fortifying that hero, turning any whispers of self-doubt into roars of self-assurance. Here, we delve into the daily habits that can enhance your mental fortitude, creating a robust foundation on which your athletic and personal achievements can soar.

4.1 Daily Habits for Stronger Mental Fortitude

Routine as a Foundation

The power of routine is immense! It brings structure to chaos and order to randomness, providing a framework that promotes mental and physical health. For you, as a teen athlete, establishing a solid daily routine is pivotal. This routine should not only encompass your training sessions but also your meals, academic work, and rest periods.

Consistency in your daily schedule reinforces discipline, reduces stress by removing unpredictability, and frees up mental space to focus on improvement in both sports and personal development. I refer to this as consistent quality or CQ.

To add routine into your schedule, start by mapping out your typical day with time blocks designated for specific activities. Prioritize your responsibilities and ensure that your training, classes, meals, and rest are planned. This doesn't mean your schedule has to be rigid. On the contrary, a good routine allows flexibility for unexpected events or shifts in mood and energy. However, having a blueprint of how your day unfolds can significantly decrease anxiety and increase productivity. Remember, the goal is to create a routine that supports your growth and aligns with your goals, not one that feels burdensome or restrictive.

Mental Skills Training

Just as you train your body, your mind requires regular workouts to build strength and endurance. Daily mental skills training can include practices like journaling, goal reviews, and mental rehearsals. Each of these activities tunes your mind for high performance, akin to how physical training conditions your body.

Journaling is a powerful tool for self-reflection and emotional management. It allows you to express thoughts and feelings in a structured way, helping to clarify goals and track progress. Each night, spend a few minutes writing about your day, focusing on what went well and what could be improved. This practice can help you keep a record of your journey, as well as helping to process emotions and experiences, reducing mental clutter and enhancing clarity.

Goal review is another crucial mental exercise. As we talked about in the previous chapter, regularly revisiting your goals is important, especially when they have to change due to circumstances outside of your control. Regularly reviewing you goals keeps them fresh in your mind, aligns your daily actions with your long-term aspirations, and provides motivation. Each morning, take a moment to remind yourself of your goals for the day and how they contribute to your bigger picture. Adjust previously set goals as needed. This alignment ensures that your daily actions are purposeful and directed toward meaningful outcomes.

Mental rehearsal, or visualization, involves mentally practicing your sport, visualizing success, and strategizing about upcoming events. We will talk more in depth about this important practice and how you can incorporate it into your routine in the next chapter.

Rest and Recovery

In the relentless pursuit of excellence, rest can often be overlooked. However, adequate rest and recovery are crucial for mental toughness. They allow your mind to recharge, process information, and consolidate skills learned during training. Ensure you get enough sleep each night, as sleep is foundational to cognitive function and emotional regulation. Additionally, integrate relaxation techniques into your routine, such as meditation, deep breathing exercises, or yoga. These practices, which we will talk more about in the next chapter, help in managing stress, reducing fatigue, and maintaining mental clarity.

Nutrition and Hydration

The adage "you are what you eat" holds profound truth, especially in the context of mental performance. Optimal nutrition supports brain function, enhances concentration, and stabilizes mood, while proper hydration ensures that your brain operates efficiently. Focus on a balanced diet rich in fruits, vegetables, lean proteins, and whole grains, and ensure you are drinking enough water throughout the day. This nutritional support is crucial not just for your physical health but for your mental well-being and resilience as well.

By incorporating these strategies into your daily routine, you create a robust framework for developing mental toughness. This toughness becomes your ally, empowering you to face the myriad challenges and pressures of teen sports with confidence and determination. As you integrate these practices into your life, they will become second nature, part of the fabric of your daily existence, enhancing your performance and your overall quality of life.

4.2 Visualization Techniques for Peak Performance

Visualization, or mental imagery, is a potent tool in an athlete's mental toolkit, one that I think is arguably the most important tool you have. It enables you to rehearse and perfect performances in the safety of your own mind before engaging in them physically in competition. This technique involves vividly imagining yourself succeeding in your sporting activities, engaging all your senses to create a detailed mental simulation of desired outcomes. Whether it's nailing the perfect dive, sprinting past the finish line, or executing a flawless soccer play, visualization reinforces neural pathways associated with your physical activities, enhancing your muscle memory even when you're not physically practicing.

To understand why mental imagery is so effective, it helps to know about the concept of functional equivalence. This psychological principle suggests that imagining performing an action activates the same neural pathways in the brain as physically performing that action. In simpler terms, when you vividly imagine executing a dive, your brain fires in very similar ways to how it would if you were actually diving. This process strengthens the neural pathways involved in the performance, making the physical execution more fluid and automatic when it actually occurs.

I had the privilege of learning mental rehearsal/visualization techniques from Dr. Robert Nideffer in the summer of 1973. Nideffer was from my hometown of Rochester, NY, and a professor at the University of Rochester. He was on the old Johnny Carson show and had just returned from the Soviet Union. While there, he had the opportunity to learn what were at the time state secrets that allowed the Russian athletes and their eastern European satellite countries to dominate the Olympics in almost every sport. I reached out to Dr. Nideffer and he graciously allowed me to come and see him and learn these key techniques.

I immediately applied them to my collegiate wrestling practices while I was at Oswego State College, and they proved successful in helping me find a focused and relaxed state. I found I was able to compete at a higher level.

Since then, I have taught them to hundreds of my wrestlers and tennis players, and they, too, have had great results staying relaxed and achieving incredible results in countless matches.

Since then, visualization has gained in popularity. For example, in 1980 I saw a big sports article on how the University of Virginia and the Dallas Cowboys had just started using the same mental rehearsal techniques. What our little school in Hancock, NY, had been doing for six years with limited resources was being replicated by major college and NFL teams.

To harness the power of visualization, start by creating a quiet, distraction-free environment where you can concentrate without interruptions. Settle into a comfortable position, close your eyes, and take a few deep breaths to center yourself. Then follow these progressive relaxation steps:

1. Take three deep breaths, as this will signal your body to move into a good mental and emotional state of relaxation.

2. Clench your fists tighter and tighter for about 5-6 seconds and then relax; feel the tension going out of your hands.

3. Repeat step 2 around 20 seconds later and have 20 seconds between each tension/relaxation exercise while continuing to breathe and relax.

4. Bring your hands and arms across your chest. Squeeze your hands and flex your biceps for 5-6 seconds and relax; feel the tension leaving them.

5. Next, with your hands open, push your arms straight out and flex your triceps for 5-6 seconds; relax and feel the tension leaving them.

6. Now, tighten your legs for 5-6 seconds and relax; feel the tension leaving.

7. Next, tighten your stomach muscles for 5-6 seconds; relax.

(These next two tension exercises are very important as much of our stress and tension begin in these two areas.)

8. Tighten your neck by pushing it back against a pillow or some other firm object. Roll it to your left for 2 seconds, straight back for 2 seconds, and to the right for 2 seconds. Relax.

9. Clench your teeth for 5-6 seconds; relax.

10. You should now be in a very relaxed alpha brain wave state. Once you are relaxed, begin by visualizing a specific athletic skill or performance that you want to improve. Picture yourself at a competition, feeling the ground under your feet, hearing the crowd's cheers, seeing the finish line ahead, and experiencing the thrill of the performance. Engage all your senses to make the experience as real as possible. The key here is consistency. The more detailed you get and the more frequently you visualize the scenario, the more ingrained it becomes in your muscle memory and subconscious, making it more likely to manifest in actual performance. Do these visualization exercises for about 10-15 minutes.

11. Once you complete these, take a couple deep breaths. You are finished.

Developing a personalized visualization routine involves setting aside regular time in your daily schedule, ideally before practice sessions or competitions. Once your body is used to these mental rehearsal sessions, it will automatically enter a focused and relaxed state ideal for a good performance with just three deep breaths. Each day you spend time on this exercise, focus on different aspects of your performance. For instance, one day you could concentrate on the start of a race and another day on the sprint and finish. Over time, these mental rehearsals can significantly boost your confidence and refine your physical performance, as your mind and body begin to align with the success scenarios you've envisioned, adding many layers to your disciplined mental toughness efforts!

Visualization also serves as a powerful antidote to performance anxiety. Before a high-pressure event, mental imagery can help calm your nerves by familiarizing you with the scenario and outcome, reducing fear of the unknown. By repeatedly visualizing successful outcomes, you train your mind to be more comfortable and confident during actual performances. If you find yourself battling pre-game jitters, take a moment to visualize not only your success but also your calm and controlled response to the competitive environment. Imagine yourself handling unexpected challenges with grace and focus, reinforcing your ability to stay composed under pressure.

As you continue to integrate visualization into your training, remember that this technique is about more than just seeing success; it's about fully immersing yourself in the experience of achievement. With regular practice, visualization can strengthen your mental resilience, enhance your performance, and equip you with the confidence to face any challenge your sport presents. As you progress, you'll find that the boundary between what you've visualized and what you can achieve becomes increasingly blurred, until they are one and the same. This seamless integration of mind and movement is the hallmark of a great athlete.

4.3 Stress-Reduction Tactics for Pre-game Anxiety

Understanding and managing pre-game anxiety is crucial for any athlete aiming to perform at their best. Anxiety before a game is a common experience; it stems from the pressure to perform, fear of failure, or even the excitement of competition. Recognizing what triggers your anxiety is the first step toward managing it effectively. These triggers can vary widely among athletes. Some might feel anxious about the outcome of the game, while others might worry about letting their team down or getting injured. Take the time to reflect on moments when you've felt anxious before a game and try to identify a pattern or specific thoughts that might be causing these feelings. This awareness allows you to address these triggers directly.

Breathing exercises are a powerful tool for managing stress and anxiety in the moment. When you're anxious, your breathing pattern changes, often leading to faster or shallower breaths, which only amplifies your sense of anxiety. Learning to control your breathing can help mitigate these feelings. One effective technique is diaphragmatic breathing, also known as deep breathing. To practice, find a quiet spot, sit comfortably, and place one hand on your belly and the other on your chest. Breathe in slowly through your nose, ensuring your belly moves more than your chest. Hold this breath for a few moments, then slowly exhale through your mouth. Repeating this exercise for a few minutes can help reduce anxiety levels significantly, calming your mind and allowing you to focus more clearly on your game.

Another technique, the "4-7-8" breathing method, where you inhale for four seconds, hold the breath for seven seconds, and exhale slowly for eight seconds, can be particularly useful in managing pre-competition nerves, helping to center your mind and body before you step into the arena.

Mental rehearsal, or visualization skills, is another key skill for managing anxiety, showing again the value the practice carries. Mastering this skill allows you to stay in the present moment, blocking out distractions around you such as the crowd, other athletes, and commentators. Calming your mind into mental focus helps you to play closer to your potential and lessens the chances of self-destructive thoughts. You can prepare well, play well, and enjoy the journey and the priceless life lessons it brings along the way.

Developing personalized pre-game routines that include physical warm-ups, mental rehearsal, listening to music, breathing exercises, or even engaging in a particular hobby that helps you relax will allow you to enter each competition feeling prepared. The key is consistency; by performing the same sequence of activities before each game, you create a sense of familiarity and control, which can be comforting when facing the uncertainties of competition. Your routine should focus on activities that leave you feeling confident, calm, and ready to tackle the game with energy and focus. For example, you could start with a light jog or stretching, followed by a few minutes of mental rehearsal where you see yourself executing perfect plays, and then wrap up with some deep breathing exercises before heading out to the field.

Creating a comprehensive plan for managing stress involves both immediate strategies for game day and long-term practices that build your overall resilience to anxiety. Proper nutrition, sleep, adequate recovery time, and engaging in mental skills training are all important long-term practices that will help you stay in a calm and controlled place. Setting aside time after games to reflect on your anxiety levels and the effectiveness of your management strategies can also help you make necessary adjustments. Over time, these reflections will enable you to develop a more intuitive understanding of your responses to stress and refine your techniques to manage them.

Implementing these strategies requires commitment and practice, but the payoff is significant. By taking control of your anxiety, you not only enhance your performance but also increase your enjoyment of the sport. Remember, the goal isn't to eliminate anxiety completely; a low level of pre-game nerves can be energizing and improve your performance. The aim is to manage anxiety so that it doesn't overwhelm you, keeping it at a level where it motivates rather than hinders. As you continue to apply these tactics, you'll likely find yourself approaching games with more confidence and a clearer mind, ready to meet the challenges of competition with poise and resilience.

4.4 Building Confidence Through Positive Self-Talk

The conversations you have with yourself are more powerful than you might realize. These internal dialogues, known as self-talk, can significantly influence your confidence, affecting everything from your daily mood to your performance in sports. Positive self-talk bolsters your confidence, pushing you toward success, while negative self-talk can pull the rug out from under you, instilling doubt and fear. Understanding how to harness the power of positive self-talk can transform how you perform, and also how you view yourself and your capabilities.

In my own training, using the G.R.I.T. acronym (Greater Results/Intense Training) in my self-talk has truly assisted in pushing out my quit point and enhancing my mental toughness. It can be done in short bursts to further assist your mental toughness journey, building self-confidence, which in turn helps to increase your ability to adapt to the challenges life will bring your way. So, how does self-talk work? Imagine you're about to try a new training technique or play in a crucial match. The thoughts running through your mind at that moment directly influence your emotional state and physical performance. Positive affirmations, such as "I can do this," calm your nerves, boost your energy, and focus your concentration, thereby enhancing your ability to perform. In contrast, negative self-talk, such as "I'm not good enough," can create a psychological barrier that hampers your performance before you even start. It can make you feel defeated, drain your energy, and divert your focus from the task at hand.

Developing the skill to recognize when negative self-talk creeps in is crucial. It often appears as doubts, criticisms, or fears that pop into your mind, typically in moments of stress or uncertainty. To counteract this, start by simply noticing these thoughts without immediately reacting to them. Awareness is the first step in transforming your self-talk. Each time a negative thought emerges, challenge its validity. For example, if you find yourself thinking, "I always mess up this routine," instead try considering the times you've succeeded at it. Then, replace that thought with a positive affirmation like, "I have the skills to do this routine well." This practice of notice, challenge, and replace gradually shifts your internal dialogue to be more encouraging and supportive.

Incorporating positive self-talk into your daily training and competition routines can further solidify its benefits. Begin each session by affirming your abilities and goals. For instance, before a training session, you might say to yourself, ""Today, I will improve my stamina and technique." Use affirmations that resonate personally with you, making them specific and realistic. During training or competitions, keep these affirmations handy in your mind, ready to counter any negative thoughts. After the events—regardless of the outcome—use positive self-talk to review your performance constructively. Focus on what you learned and how you can improve, rather than what went wrong. This helps in building resilience and also prepares you better for future challenges.

By consistently practicing and reinforcing positive dialogue, you can significantly enhance your self-confidence and performance. Remember, the goal of positive self-talk isn't to deny or ignore the challenges you face but to approach them with a mindset that promotes confidence and resilience. As you continue to develop this skill, you'll find that the benefits extend beyond sports, enriching all areas of your life with greater positivity and self-assurance.

4.5 Overcoming Fear of Failure On and Off the Field

Fear of failure is a shadow that looms over many athletes, from the fields of local high schools to the grand arenas of professional sports. This fear isn't just about a single missed goal or a lost match; it digs deeper, tapping into the worry that you're not enough, that your efforts won't measure up, and that your mistakes will define you. Understanding this fear is the first step in conquering it. It often stems from a combination of high personal expectations and the perceived pressure from coaches, peers, and the specter of public scrutiny. These pressures can make the prospect of failure seem catastrophic, overshadowing the intrinsic joy and personal growth that sports can foster.

Recognizing the roots of this fear will allow you to address it more effectively. It's crucial to acknowledge that feeling scared of falling short is a part of being human, particularly in competitive environments. However, the impact of this fear can be profound, potentially stifling your willingness to take necessary risks and try new strategies, which are essential for growth and improvement. It can lead to a conservative approach in training and competitions, where you might hold back rather than push through your personal quit point. This restraint can hinder both performance and personal development, as growth often requires stepping out of comfort zones and facing the unknown with determination.

Reframing failure is a transformative technique that can change your entire outlook on sports and competition. Instead of viewing failure as a negative endpoint, see it as an integral part of learning and mastery. Every misstep gives you valuable information about what doesn't work, guiding you on how to adjust and improve. Embracing this perspective involves a shift in your internal dialogue and a reevaluation of how you define success and failure. For instance, instead of berating yourself for not securing a win, focus on the skills you improved during the game or what the experience taught you about your strategy and resilience. This shift doesn't stop the disappointment of failure but places it in a context where it can be used constructively, fueling rather than hindering your drive to improve.

Encouraging calculated risk-taking is another vital aspect of overcoming the fear of failure. In training and competition, taking risks can lead to significant breakthroughs in your performance. Whether it's trying a new technique in a game or setting a more challenging pace in practice, these risks push you beyond your current boundaries, which is where growth happens. Coaches play a crucial role in fostering a safe environment for taking these risks. They can create training situations that stretch your abilities and provide immediate, constructive feedback, helping you learn from the experience, regardless of the outcome. This support not only boosts your confidence but also demystifies the act of taking risks, making it a normal, managed part of your athletic development.

Your support system—coaches, teammates, family—is indispensable in transforming how you handle failure and fear. These individuals can offer encouragement, share their own experiences with setbacks, and provide perspective that can help you see beyond the immediate impact of failure. A supportive coach can remind you of your progress and potential, a teammate can empathize with your experience, offering solidarity, and family members can provide the unconditional support that reassures you of your value, independent of your athletic performance. This network of support is crucial, not just for coping with failure when it happens but for building the resilience and confidence that preempt fear of failure.

As we wrap up this exploration into the strategies for enhancing mental toughness, remember that the journey doesn't end here. Each step you take builds upon the last, creating a path of growth, learning, and resilience that extends beyond sports. The lessons learned in overcoming fear, managing stress, and building confidence are tools that will serve you well in all arenas of life. I firmly believe the key advantages of competitive sports are found in these priceless life lessons. In learning these, the advantage you will have will put you well ahead of most of the competition, and especially those too timid to step out and compete. Your fitness level will allow for more energy, which in turn will allow you to accomplish more each day, resulting in positive feelings of satisfaction. This continues to build, as feeling good about yourself improves your self-image, which leads you to perform better in your sport. These lessons also allow those who are developing self-reliance in their lives to hold a marketable skill, which will improve your life outside of sports. Chasing self-reliance with energy and a solid work ethic, along with connecting with key people through excellent communication skills, will allow you to live a life well-lived as you use your skills and talents for the benefit of others.

The insights gained here set the stage for the next chapter, where we explore the mind-body connection, diving deeper into how integrating training strategies that incorporate mental and physical training into your routine can further elevate your athletic prowess.

Chapter 5

The Mind-Body Connection: Techniques to Enhance Both

Imagine stepping onto the field or court not just with physical readiness but with a profound connection between your mind and body, each movement and decision flowing seamlessly from one to the next. This chapter is about turning that vision into reality, leveraging practices that have stood the test of time to enhance your athletic prowess and mental clarity. Here, we explore how the practices of yoga and Pilates, along with the restorative practices of meditation and mindfulness, can be more than just exercises; they can be transformative tools that intertwine your physical and mental capacities, making you a more formidable, focused, and resilient athlete.

5.1 Yoga and Pilates for Athletes: Strengthening the Mind-Body Link

Benefits for Athletes

Yoga and Pilates, often perceived merely as supplementary exercises, hold a treasure trove of benefits that can revolutionize the way you engage with your sport. For starters, both practices excel in enhancing flexibility. This isn't just about touching your toes or twisting into complex poses; it's about reducing the risk of injuries by helping your muscles and joints move through their full range of motion. Enhanced flexibility ensures that sudden, sharp movements during a game are less likely to result in a strain or tear.

Balance and core strength are other critical areas where yoga and Pilates shine. These disciplines focus on stabilizing and strengthening your core, the central part of your body that dictates how well you can control and move your limbs. A strong core improves your athletic performance through increasing your overall stability, ensuring that every jump, run, or swing is executed with precision.

The mental benefits are also substantial. Regular practice of yoga and Pilates can lead to significant reductions in stress and anxiety, thanks to their meditative elements that help you focus on the present moment and clear your mind of distractions. This enhanced mental focus is crucial during competitions, where a clear head can make the difference between a win and a loss.

Incorporating into Training

Integrating yoga and Pilates into your training regime won't require an overhaul of your entire schedule. Instead, it's about finding pockets of time where these practices can enhance your existing routines. For instance, incorporating a twenty-minute yoga session into your warm-up can prepare both your mind and body for the rigors ahead, making your muscles more pliable and your mind more focused. A Pilates session could serve as an excellent cool-down, helping to ease your body back into a state of rest and recovery after intense physical exertion.

The frequency and timing of these sessions can vary based on your sport and personal needs. However, a good rule of thumb is to practice yoga or Pilates at least twice a week. This frequency ensures that you gain the flexibility and mental benefits without overwhelming your schedule. Early morning, when the mind is still fresh and uncluttered, is an ideal time because it sets a tone of calm and control that can benefit you throughout the day.

Targeted Practices for Athletes

Not all yoga poses or Pilates exercises are created equal, especially when it comes to meeting the specific needs of athletes. Certain poses and exercises can be particularly beneficial, depending on the sports you engage in. For example, runners may benefit immensely from "Pigeon Pose" in yoga, which can help release tension in the hip flexors and lower back, areas often strained in long-distance running. Similarly, "The Hundred"—a classic Pilates exercise—can be a game-changer by strengthening the abdominal muscles and improving lung capacity, which is crucial for almost any sport.

It's also wise to focus on exercises that prevent common sports injuries. For basketball players or other athletes involved in sports requiring a lot of jumping, strengthening the knee joints and improving balance can help prevent the dreaded ACL injuries. Yoga poses like "Warrior III" and Pilates exercises like "Leg Circles" can fortify these areas by enhancing stability and strengthening the muscles around the knees.

Mind-Body Awareness

Perhaps the most profound benefit of integrating yoga and Pilates into your athletic training is the enhanced mind-body awareness. This awareness, cultivated through focused movements and controlled breathing, teaches you to understand the signals your body sends you, which can be crucial in avoiding overtraining or recognizing when an injury is looming. It not only helps in maintaining peak physical condition but also fosters a deeper understanding of how mental states can affect physical performance. Learning to control your breathing, staying present during practice, and moving intentionally translate directly into better performance during games or competitions, where mental clarity and physical control are paramount.

5.2 The Role of Meditation in Athletic Recovery

Meditation, often associated with a sense of calm and tranquility, has been seen to have a wide variety of benefits that cover many aspects of sports, particularly in recovery. Engaging in meditation can significantly accelerate your recovery times, enhance your sleep quality, and reduce stress levels, making it an invaluable tool in your athletic arsenal. When you meditate, you engage in a deliberate practice that enhances your ability to regulate emotions and maintain calmness under pressure, qualities that are beneficial both on and off the field.

One of the primary benefits of meditation for athletes is its profound impact on stress reduction. Training and competition can place considerable stress on your body and mind, and without proper management, this stress can impair your recovery and overall performance. Meditation activates the parasympathetic nervous system—the part of your autonomic nervous system responsible for relaxation and regeneration. By doing so, it facilitates processes that are critical for recovery, such as muscle repair and toxin elimination.

Meditation has also been shown to improve the quality of sleep, a critical element of recovery. Deep, restorative sleep accelerates physical repair, fortifies mental health, and improves cognitive functions like decision-making and focus. By incorporating meditation into your routine, you can enhance these recovery processes, ensuring you are ready and at your best for each training session or competition.

Introducing meditation into your athletic training can be as simple as dedicating a few minutes before bed to practice mindfulness meditation, which involves paying attention to your breath and being present in the moment. This practice can help you unwind and disconnect from the day's stresses, preparing you for a restful night's sleep. Alternatively, engaging in guided meditations post-training can help shift your body into a state of deep relaxation and recovery. You can ask your coach for some ideas on how to begin incorporating meditation into your routine or for resources that will help. The key is consistency; regular practice amplifies the benefits, helping you manage stress, maintain mental clarity, and recover faster.

Different meditation techniques offer various benefits, and finding the one that works best for you can be a game changer. Mindfulness meditation, as mentioned, is fantastic for cultivating a state of awareness and presence, invaluable during high-pressure moments in sports. Guided meditation, where a voice leads you through a series of relaxing visualizations or instructions, can be particularly beneficial for those who find it difficult to focus or relax. This type of meditation can be tailored to address specific areas such as pain management, stress reduction, or performance anxiety. Visualization meditation, another powerful technique, involves envisioning yourself succeeding in your sport, executing perfect movements, or overcoming a challenging situation. This technique not only aids in recovery but also prepares your mind for future performances, embedding a sense of confidence and readiness.

5.3 Integrating Mindfulness into Physical Training

Mindfulness, at its core, involves maintaining a moment-by-moment awareness of our thoughts, feelings, bodily sensations, and surrounding environment through a gentle, nurturing lens. When applied to athletic training, mindfulness transcends the basic act of physical exertion, transforming routine exercises into a rich, engaging experience that enhances both the mind and body.

The application of mindfulness in athletic training can significantly sharpen your focus. The ability to focus longer than your opponents will give you a considerable edge. This heightened focus is crucial during both practice and competition, allowing you to maintain concentration on your technique and strategy without distraction. For instance, during a high-pressure game or match, a mindful athlete can remain calm and focused, effectively tuning out distractions and channeling their energy toward optimal performance. This ability to stay present not only enhances performance but also increases the enjoyment of the sport, as you become more engaged and less mechanically involved in the activity.

Integrating mindfulness into your training isn't complex but requires consistent practice. One effective way to cultivate mindfulness is through mindful running or mindful strength training. During mindful running, instead of simply clocking miles, focus on the sensation of your feet touching the ground, the rhythm of your breath, and the feeling of the wind against your face. This practice improves your physical endurance and reduces the stress often associated with long-distance running. Similarly, during strength training, instead of rapidly moving through sets, concentrate on the muscle groups you are working. Feel each muscle contract and relax, and align your breathing with your movements. Doing this enhances your technique and, at the same time, fosters a greater awareness of the body's needs and limits, minimizing the risk of injury. By understanding and respecting these limits, you ensure that your training enhances your strength and endurance without compromising your well-being.

The benefits of incorporating mindfulness into your training regimen extend beyond improved performance and enjoyment. Mindful athletes often experience better mental health, as regular mindfulness practice has been shown to reduce symptoms of stress, anxiety, and depression. By learning to manage stress effectively through mindfulness, you can maintain a clearer mental state, which is invaluable in both training and recovery phases. Creating a training environment that supports mindfulness is crucial for cultivating these benefits. Begin by minimizing distractions in your training environment. This might mean choosing a quieter time for your workouts or creating a dedicated space in your home where you can train without interruptions. Setting intentional goals for each training session can also enhance mindfulness. Before beginning your workout, take a few moments to clarify what you wish to achieve and why it matters to you. This practice not only sets a purposeful tone for the session but also aligns your mind and body towards achieving these goals.

Additionally, fostering a supportive community plays a significant role in maintaining a mindful approach. Training with peers who value and practice mindfulness can reinforce your own practice. Share techniques and experiences, and support each other in cultivating mindfulness during training sessions. In essence, integrating mindfulness into your physical training transforms it from a routine task into a holistic growth experience, where every run, swim, stroke, or lift becomes an opportunity to connect deeply with yourself and your environment. This connection is what makes you a stronger athlete and a more resilient individual. As you continue to explore and integrate mindfulness into your training, carry forward the understanding that your greatest strength lies not only in the physical prowess you display but also in the mindful presence you bring to each moment of your athletic journey.

In this chapter, we've explored how mindfulness can transform your training, enhancing your focus, performance, and enjoyment of sports. As you move forward, remember that each step, stroke, or stretch is an opportunity to practice mindfulness, deepening your connection to both your sport and yourself, setting the stage for continued growth and achievement in all areas of life.

Looking ahead, the next chapter will focus on customizing fitness routines to maximize physical health and athletic performance, complementing the mental skills you've developed with physical strategies to further your journey as a well-rounded athlete.

Chapter 6

Customized Fitness Routines Post-Covid

As we navigated the shifting landscapes that the COVID-19 pandemic sculpted around our lives, particularly in the realm of sports and fitness, the need for adaptability was never clearer. For you, the aspiring teen athlete, this era presented unique challenges but also unique opportunities. The disruption of traditional training environments and schedules demanded a fresh approach, one that respected the new norms but also pushed the boundaries of what could be achieved within them.

This chapter is about taking those lessons learned during the pandemic so that we can continue to empower your fitness routine in a way that helps you to reach and perhaps even exceed your pre-pandemic peak performance. These workouts will focus on efficiency in your workouts, ensuring they pack a punch in limited time and space, and are also customized to fit your individual athletic needs and circumstances.

6.1 Designing a 40-Minute High-Impact Workout for Teen Athletes

Efficiency and Effectiveness

In today's fast-paced world, where school, social activities, and perhaps even part-time jobs vie for your attention, efficiency in training is paramount. A 40-minute workout, crafted thoughtfully, can not only fit into your busy schedule but also deliver the intensity and effectiveness needed to enhance athletic performance. The key is focusing on quality over quantity, ensuring that every minute of your workout is purposeful and contributes directly to your athletic development. This approach respects your time constraints and also challenges you to push your limits within a compact timeframe, which can lead to significant improvements in your fitness levels.

Workout Components

A well-rounded 40-minute workout for teen athletes like yourself should include several key components: warm-up, high-intensity interval training (HIIT), strength training, and cool-down. Each segment plays a crucial role in maximizing the workout's effectiveness and preventing injuries.

- **Warm-up:** Begin with a 5-minute dynamic warm-up to prepare your body for the intense activity ahead. This could include activities like jumping jacks, leg swings, and arm circles, which increase your heart rate and loosen up your muscles.

- **High-Intensity Interval Training (HIIT):** Spend about 20 minutes on HIIT, which is incredibly effective for improving cardiovascular fitness, speed, and endurance. Incorporate exercises like sprints, burpees, and high knees. The key is to alternate between periods of intense activity and short recovery periods.

- **Strength Training**: Dedicate 10 minutes to strength training, focusing on major muscle groups. Use body-weight exercises like push-ups, planks, and lunges, which can be performed anywhere, without the need for gym equipment.

- **Cool-down**: Conclude with a 5-minute cool-down to help your body recover and prevent muscle stiffness. Gentle stretching and breathing exercises can aid in this process, helping to relax your muscles and bring your heart rate back down.

Customization Tips

Customizing your workout is essential to address your specific sports requirements and fitness level. If you're a sprinter, for instance, your HIIT segments might focus more on short bursts of running with very brief rest periods. If you're into sports like soccer or basketball, incorporating agility drills that mimic in-game movements can be beneficial. Always consider your current fitness level as well; if you're just starting out, you might need longer rest intervals in your HIIT workouts. As you progress, you can increase the intensity and decrease the rest periods.

6.2 Safety Guidelines: Injury Prevention and Recovery

While pushing your limits is part of improving athletic performance, ensuring the safety of your workouts is crucial. Always prioritize proper form over the number of repetitions to prevent injuries. Gradual progression in the intensity of your workouts can also help your body adapt without undue risk, enhancing your athletic capabilities safely over time. If you're unsure about the correct form, seek advice from a coach or watch instructional videos from reliable sources. Additionally, ensure your workout space is safe—sufficiently spacious and free from potential hazards. It's not just about continuing to train but doing so in a way that safeguards your body, ensuring longevity in your sport of choice. In this context, dynamic warm-ups, proper cooldowns, and holistic safety methods aren't just beneficial; they're essential components of a safe and effective personal training regime.

Dynamic Warm-Ups

Dynamic warm-ups serve as the cornerstone of injury prevention. Unlike static stretching, which involves holding a stretch for a long period, dynamic warm-ups involve movement-based stretches that mimic the activity you will be doing. For example, if you're a runner, this could include leg swings, walking lunges, or arm circles. These exercises increase blood flow to the muscles and joints, enhance neurological awareness, and reduce stiffness, which collectively help to decrease your risk of injuries during more intense physical activities. Mobility exercises also play a significant role because they help maintain joint health and functional range of motion. Incorporating tools like resistance bands for leg and arm stretches or doing body-weight movements such as hip circles and shoulder shrugs can keep you limber and less prone to injuries that stem from rigid muscles and joints.

Cooldowns

In addition to warm-ups and mobility work, proper cooldowns are vital. After your main workout session, gradually winding down with activities like slow jogging or walking followed by stretches similar to your warm-up routine helps in gradually lowering heart rates, cooling down the body, and reducing muscle stiffness. This gradual transition is crucial in regulating blood flow, which can prevent dizziness or fainting, and also helps to flush out toxins from the muscles, reducing soreness and speeding up recovery.

Solo recovery techniques gained prominence during the pandemic because of limitations on professional medical consultations and physiotherapy sessions. Self-administered recovery methods such as foam rolling and restorative yoga can be highly effective. Foam rolling, for instance, helps in breaking down muscle knots and promoting blood flow to different muscle groups, which can speed up recovery and improve performance. It's a form of self-myofascial release that can be incredibly beneficial after high-intensity training. Restorative yoga, on the other hand, focuses on deep relaxation and stretching. Poses like the legs-up-the-wall or gentle spinal twists can help in aligning your body post-training, promoting recovery and reducing the risk of injuries.

Holistic Safety Guidelines

Building resilience against injuries isn't solely about physical precautions; it also encompasses a holistic approach that includes balanced training schedules, adequate nutrition, and sufficient rest. Ensuring that your body gets the necessary nutrients to repair itself after workouts is critical. Protein for muscle repair, carbohydrates for energy replenishment, and fats for inflammation reduction are all vital. Hydration is another key factor; it aids in joint lubrication, temperature regulation, and nutrient transport within the body. We will talk more about nutrition and hydration in the next chapter, so that you are armed with practical tools for enhancing your nutritional power.

By integrating these practices into your routine, you take charge of your own athletic health and development. It also helps you grow in self-reliance, as no one should care more about your own self care than *you*! As you continue to navigate your training journey, remember that each step you take in injury prevention and recovery is a step toward a more robust and sustainable athletic career.

6.3 ADAPTING TRAINING FOR LIMITED ACCESS TO FACILITIES

During the pandemic, when access to traditional training facilities was limited or fluctuating due to ongoing health concerns, your adaptability as an athlete was more crucial than ever. If you wanted your athletic progress to remain uninterrupted even in less-than-ideal conditions, it demanded creativity and resourcefulness from you.

So, why are we talking about this again now? In reflecting on the lessons we learned from the pandemic, we can understand how to fully dive into mental toughness for any future changes to our normal routines. We can prepare ourselves now for what is ahead. The ability to adapt your training regimen to the confines of limited space and equipment is not just a necessity but a skill that will continue to serve you well throughout your athletic career.

Creative Use of Space and Equipment

Firstly, when space becomes an issue, it's important to understand how you can transform your immediate environment into a functional training area. Every space around you holds potential; it's about viewing it through a creative lens. For instance, stairs can double as a tool for cardio workouts—running up and down can be a potent exercise for building endurance and leg strength. Similarly, a sturdy chair or bench can support exercises like step-ups, tricep dips, or incline push-ups. Look around your home or neighborhood: a wall can be used for wall sits, a heavy backpack can replace weights for squats or lunges, and even a hallway can become a sprint lane.

Public parks and playgrounds can also offer a number of workout possibilities. During the pandemic, I used the local park for dips between two picnic tables, did chin ups and leg raises on the jungle gym, and completed pushups with my feet up on a park bench. Park benches are also perfect for box jumps and split squats, while monkey bars are excellent for pull-ups and hanging leg raises. Open fields are ideal for agility drills using cones or makeshift markers.

Embrace these opportunities, and you'll find that your environment is rich with possibilities for maintaining an effective training regimen. This approach not only ensures continuity in your physical training but also sharpens your problem-solving skills and enhances your adaptability—qualities that are invaluable in sports and life.

Bodyweight Training

Bodyweight training is a highly effective method that utilizes your own body's weight as resistance. The beauty of bodyweight exercises lies in their simplicity and the minimal requirement of space and equipment, making them perfect for situations where access to gym facilities is limited. Exercises like push-ups, sit-ups, planks, and squats can be performed almost anywhere and can be modified to increase or decrease difficulty levels. For instance, elevating your feet can increase the intensity of traditional push-ups, while slowing down the pace of your squats can enhance muscle endurance.

The versatility of bodyweight training also allows you to tailor your workouts to specific athletic goals. If flexibility and balance are your focus, integrating movements like yoga poses or Pilates exercises can be beneficial. These exercises strengthen muscles and also improve joint mobility and balance, which are crucial for nearly all sports. Regular engagement in bodyweight training not only maintains your physical condition but also ensures a balanced development of muscle groups, reducing the risk of injuries and improving overall athletic performance.

Sport-Specific Drills

Adapting sport-specific drills to smaller spaces or individual practice is another challenge that requires creativity. For sports like basketball or soccer, you can use a small area to practice dribbling or footwork drills. Set up mini-obstacles or markers to simulate game situations, or use a wall for practicing passing and shooting. For track and field athletes, short sprints combined with agility drills like ladder runs or cone drills can simulate the explosive movements needed during races.

Creating variations of these drills to keep them challenging and engaging is crucial. For instance, altering the speed, intensity, or complexity of the drills over time can help in continuously challenging your skills and preventing plateauing, which is crucial for maintaining high levels of motivation.

6.4 Integrating Home Workouts for Strength and Flexibility

When designing home workouts that effectively target both strength and flexibility, it's crucial to understand that these elements are the pillars upon which athletic performance is built. A balanced routine that includes both can significantly enhance your capabilities across a variety of sports and activities, contributing to a well-rounded athletic profile. To create a home workout that integrates these components, start by defining a clear structure that alternates between strength and flexibility exercises. This approach ensures that you are building muscle and enhancing your power output at the same time as improving your range of motion and reducing the risk of injury.

For a well-rounded session, begin with a light warm-up to get your blood flowing—think jumping jacks or a brisk walk. Following this, you might engage in a circuit of bodyweight exercises designed to build strength, such as push-ups, squats, and lunges. Each exercise should be performed for a set number of repetitions or time intervals, ensuring that you are challenging your muscles sufficiently to promote growth and endurance. Once you've completed a round of these strength exercises, shift your focus to flexibility. This part of the workout could include dynamic stretches such as leg swings and arm sweeps, which help maintain and extend your range of motion and prepare your muscles for the next round of intensive exercise.

To enhance your strength training without traditional weights, consider innovative methods like using resistance bands or creating homemade weights with common household items like filled water bottles or sandbags. Resistance bands, for example, can be used to add an extra level of challenge to bodyweight exercises. Wrap them around your legs during squats or under your feet for bicep curls, and you'll feel an increase in resistance that mimics the effect of lifting weights. These tools are not only effective but also versatile and easy to store, making them perfect for home workout environments where space and equipment might be limited.

Incorporating flexibility training into your routine is not just about performing stretches at the end of your workout session. To truly benefit from increased flexibility, you should integrate it throughout your session. This can be achieved through the inclusion of exercises that promote a greater range of motion, such as yoga poses or Pilates movements, which can be interspersed with more traditional strength exercises. For instance, after a set of push-ups, you might transition into a child's pose to stretch your back and shoulders, or follow a series of lunges with a warrior pose to deepen the stretch in your hips and thighs.

Maintaining a variety of exercises in your routine is critical to preventing boredom and ensuring holistic development. Regularly update your workout plan to include new exercises, challenge different muscle groups, and keep your mind engaged. This might mean trying out a new yoga routine, experimenting with Pilates, or switching up the type of resistance used in your strength exercises. This variability helps prevent physical plateaus, while keeping you mentally stimulated and committed to your fitness regime.

By thoughtfully integrating strength and flexibility exercises, using creative tools and methods, and regularly introducing new challenges into your routine, your home workouts can remain dynamic, effective, and rewarding. These sessions will not only help you build the physical qualities necessary for athletic success but also ensure you maintain the motivation and enthusiasm essential for long-term engagement in sports and fitness. As you continue to adapt and evolve your home workout regimen, embrace the flexibility and creativity this space offers, and use it to explore new dimensions of your athletic potential.

6.5 The Importance of Rest and Active Recovery

Understanding the balance between exertion and recovery is crucial, especially in a world where the mantra often seems to be "more is better." For you as an athlete, rest and recovery are not just downtime but essential components of an effective training program. They allow your body to heal and strengthen, and equally importantly, they rejuvenate your mind, giving you the mental clarity and resilience needed to meet your training demands effectively.

I over-trained throughout high school but learned in college the vital need for quality rest and recovery. Once I started implementing these important lessons, as well as learning the skills I needed to peak physically, mentally, and emotionally, my consistent and improved performance rose to higher and higher levels.

Rest days and active recovery play both pivotal roles in your training cycle. Physiologically, rest helps in the repair of tissues damaged during rigorous workouts, while also allowing your muscles to replenish their glycogen stores, which are your body's primary energy source during high-intensity activities. Psychologically, taking a break can prevent mental burnout, keeping you motivated and focused. It's essential to integrate complete rest days and active recovery days into your routine, ensuring that these are planned strategically to align with your training intensity and competition schedule.

Active recovery refers to engaging in low-intensity exercise on your rest days, which can help maintain a level of slight activity without overstressing your body. Activities like walking, gentle cycling, or swimming are ideal, as they increase blood circulation, helping to remove toxins built up during intense workouts and delivering nutrients needed for repair. Incorporating these kinds of activities into your weekly routine aids in physical recovery and also keeps your body active, helping to maintain a routine that can psychologically prepare you for more intense sessions ahead.

Recognizing the signs of overtraining is crucial for any athlete, and it's something you need to be keenly aware of. Symptoms can be subtle and creep up gradually, making them easy to overlook until they significantly impact your health and performance. Physical signs include prolonged muscle soreness that doesn't improve with rest, increased incidence of injuries, insomnia, and a decrease in performance despite intense training. Psychological signs might include feeling irritable, depressed, or losing interest in the sport altogether. These symptoms suggest that your body is not recovering adequately between training sessions, leading to a decrease in performance and an increased risk of injuries. By listening to your body and acknowledging these warning signs, you can adjust your training and recovery strategies to maintain your health and athletic performance.

Positioning recovery as an integral part of your training involves understanding its impact on your performance. Recovery should not be reactive but a proactive part of your training plan. This means scheduling regular rest days, engaging in active recovery sessions, and paying attention to your body's response to training loads. By integrating these practices into your training, you will set a foundation for sustained athletic performance. Recovery is as critical as the workouts themselves and should be treated with the same seriousness and planning. Remember, optimal performance is achieved not just by pushing your limits but by balancing exertion with recovery. This understanding will help you achieve your current athletic goals and also ensure a long, healthy sporting career.

Moving forward, the next chapter will focus on optimizing your nutrition for peak athletic performance. We'll explore how the right dietary choices can fuel your body for both training and recovery, setting you up for success in all your athletic endeavors.

Chapter 7

Nutrition for Peak Performance

As you dive into the world of competitive sports and rigorous training schedules, understanding the foundational role of nutrition is essential. Think of your body as a high-performance engine. Just as premium fuel can enhance the efficiency and output of a sports car, the right nutrition can significantly boost your physical performance and recovery. This chapter is about fueling your journey toward becoming a formidable athlete; one who is equipped to face the intense demands of your sport with vigor and resilience.

7.1 FUELING YOUR BODY: NUTRITION BASICS FOR TEEN ATHLETES

Balanced Diet Fundamentals

At the core of peak athletic performance lies a well-balanced diet that caters specifically to your needs as a teen athlete. This diet is structured around three major components: macronutrients (carbohydrates, proteins, and fats), micronutrients (vitamins and minerals), and adequate caloric intake to meet energy expenditures. Carbohydrates are your body's primary fuel source, especially necessary for high-intensity training, as they are converted into glucose and stored in your muscles as glycogen. When you exercise, your body taps into these glycogen reserves for energy, making adequate carbohydrate intake crucial.

Proteins, on the other hand, are essential for the repair and growth of muscle tissues that undergo wear and tear during training. A sufficient protein intake ensures you recover properly and gain muscle strength.

Healthy fats are equally important, but often overlooked, providing a concentrated source of energy and essential fatty acids that play a crucial role in hormonal functions, including those that regulate inflammation and immune health.

Micronutrients, which include a variety of vitamins and minerals, though needed in smaller quantities, are vital for energy production, injury prevention, and overall health. Iron, calcium, and vitamin D are particularly important for teen athletes. Iron helps in transporting oxygen to your muscles, calcium is crucial for bone health, and vitamin D aids in calcium absorption and muscle function. Ensuring a diet rich in these nutrients can significantly enhance your performance and prevent injuries.

Timing of Meals

The timing of your meals is crucial in aligning your nutritional intake with your body's energy needs. Eating the right foods at the right time can optimize your energy levels and recovery. A hearty breakfast jumpstarts your metabolism and replenishes glycogen stores, providing the energy needed for morning training. Eating carbohydrates and protein within forty-five minutes after training, often referred to as the anabolic window, maximizes muscle recovery and growth. Additionally, small, balanced snacks between meals can maintain your energy levels throughout the day, preventing the peaks and valleys in blood sugar that can affect your mood and energy.

Eating for Energy

To support your demanding training schedule, incorporate energy-dense meals and snacks that pack more calories and nutrients into less volume. Smoothies are a great example; blending fruits with yogurt or a protein source like whey, adding a handful of spinach, and a tablespoon of flaxseeds can provide a balanced mix of macronutrients along with essential vitamins and minerals. For snacks, think of combining complex carbohydrates with proteins: apple slices with peanut butter, a small handful of nuts with raisins, or a whole-grain cereal bar with a glass of milk. These combinations provide sustained energy that helps you stay at the top of your game.

Nutritional Challenges

Teen athletes often face unique nutritional challenges, such as balancing their energy needs with their busy academic and social lives. Skipping meals or relying on fast food can lead to suboptimal nutrient intake, which might impair your performance and recovery. To combat this, planning is key. Prepare nutrient-rich, simple meals and snacks ahead of time. Keep healthy snacks readily available in your backpack or sports bag. Engaging in meal prep on weekends can ensure you have access to healthy meals throughout the week, making it easier to fuel your body adequately, no matter how hectic your schedule gets.

By understanding and applying these nutritional fundamentals, you equip yourself with the knowledge to make informed choices about what, when, and how much to eat. This helps to support your athletic performance and enhances your overall well-being, providing the energy and nutrients needed to excel both in sports and in life. As you move forward, remember that nutrition is a powerful tool in your arsenal as an athlete, one that requires attention and respect. It's not just about eating; it's about fueling your journey toward athletic excellence.

7.2 HYDRATION STRATEGIES FOR ENHANCED PERFORMANCE

Hydration plays an indispensable role in your performance as an athlete, influencing everything from your physical endurance to your ability to recover after intense workouts. Proper hydration affects your body's ability to regulate temperature, keep joints lubricated, and transport nutrients to give you energy and keep you healthy. When you're well-hydrated, your heart pumps blood more efficiently, allowing oxygen and other essential nutrients to reach your muscles and organs, optimizing your performance and resilience. On the flip side, even mild dehydration can hinder your athletic abilities, leading to decreased coordination, muscle fatigue, and, in severe cases, heat exhaustion.

Understanding your personal hydration needs is crucial, as these can vary greatly depending on a multitude of factors, including the intensity of your activity, the climate, and your individual physiology. A simple yet effective way to monitor your hydration status is to check the color of your urine. Light, pale yellow urine typically indicates proper hydration, whereas a dark yellow or amber color suggests dehydration. Additionally, paying attention to how much you sweat during exercise can give you a clue about how much fluid you're losing and need to replace. Some athletes weigh themselves before and after workouts to measure water loss—every pound lost equates to about sixteen ounces of fluid that needs to be replenished.

To maintain optimal hydration before, during, and after your training sessions or competitions, you should develop a hydration strategy that begins well before you start sweating. About two to three hours before exercise, try to drink seventeen to twenty ounces of water. Then, around twenty to thirty minutes before starting, drink another eight ounces. During the activity, aim to consume seven to ten ounces of fluid every ten to twenty minutes, adjusting based on your sweat rate, the activity intensity, and environmental conditions. After the activity, focus on replenishing any fluid lost. A helpful tip is to drink sixteen to twenty-four ounces of fluid for every pound of body weight lost during exercise.

Electrolytes—including sodium, potassium, calcium, and magnesium—play a critical role in how your body manages hydration. They help maintain fluid balance, muscle contractions, and nerve signals. Most sports drinks contain these electrolytes and can help replenish what is lost during intense workouts, especially activities lasting longer than an hour or completed in hot conditions. However, it's important not to overdo it with these drinks, as they can contain high levels of sugars. Alternatives like coconut water can be a good source of electrolytes with less sugar. For those engaged in prolonged and strenuous activities, having a salty snack or adding a little salt to your water can also help maintain the necessary balance of electrolytes, especially if you tend to sweat profusely.

Maintaining proper hydration and electrolyte balance isn't just a strategy for maximizing your current training session—it's a long-term commitment to your health and athletic performance. The habits you build now around hydration will help you sustain high levels of performance, minimize your risk of injury, and recover more effectively, keeping you on track toward achieving and surpassing your athletic goals. As you continue to train and compete, keep these hydration strategies in mind, tweaking and adjusting based on your experiences and needs, and you'll find that optimum hydration becomes second nature, supporting every stride, swing, and sprint in your athletic journey.

7.3 Supplementation: What Works and What Doesn't

Navigating the world of dietary supplements can be like finding your way through a labyrinth filled with promises of quick results and enhanced performance. As an athlete, the allure of supplements that might improve your strength, speed, and recovery is hard to ignore. However, not all supplements are created equal, and some can do more harm than good. Before you consider adding any supplement to your diet, it's crucial to assess whether it's necessary and how it might impact your health and athletic performance.

Evaluating your supplement needs should start with a thorough analysis of your current diet and an understanding of your specific athletic demands. Supplements should not replace a balanced diet but rather fill in the gaps. For instance, if you're consistently missing out on crucial nutrients like iron or calcium, which are vital for athletic performance, supplementation might be beneficial. Similarly, if your training regimen is particularly grueling, you might require more protein than your current diet provides, making a protein supplement worth considering. However, the decision to supplement should always be based on a real, identified nutritional deficiency rather than a general desire to boost performance.

When it comes to the efficacy of supplements, sticking to those supported by scientific research is key. For example, creatine is widely studied and has been consistently shown to improve high-intensity exercise capacity and increase muscle mass in some athletes. Beta-alanine, another well-researched supplement, can benefit performance during high-intensity and endurance activities by buffering acid in muscles. However, it's important to note that the response to supplements can be highly individual. Just because a supplement works for one athlete doesn't mean it will have the same effect on another. This variability underscores the importance of approaching supplementation with a critical mind and specific goals, rather than following trends or peer recommendations without further investigation.

The risks associated with unsupervised supplementation cannot be overstated. The supplement industry is not as tightly regulated as the pharmaceutical industry, which can lead to inconsistencies in the quality and purity of products. Some supplements may contain substances that are not listed on their labels, which can pose health risks or lead to a positive doping test. Therefore, choosing products that are third-party tested and certified by reputable organizations such as NSF International or Informed-Sport is crucial. These certifications help ensure that the supplement actually contains what it claims to contain and is free of banned substances.

Lastly, consulting with healthcare providers or sports nutritionists before starting any supplement regimen is essential. These professionals can help you understand your specific needs, recommend reputable products, and monitor your health while you're using supplements. They can also keep you informed about any potential interactions between supplements and medications you might be taking or other unforeseen side effects. This step is not just a precaution but a critical component of responsible supplement use, ensuring that your path toward enhanced athletic performance does not compromise your health.

By approaching supplementation with a well-informed and cautious mindset, you can make choices that genuinely benefit your health and athletic performance. Remember, supplements can be a valuable tool when used correctly, but they are just one piece of the puzzle. A balanced diet, proper hydration, adequate rest, and rigorous training are equally, if not more, important to reaching your peak performance. As you continue to navigate your athletic development, keep these factors in balance, and always prioritize your health and well-being in the pursuit of your sporting goals.

7.4 Eating for Recovery: Post-workout Nutrition

Understanding the critical role of post-workout nutrition can significantly influence your recovery and overall athletic performance. The primary goals after any intense workout involve replenishing your energy stores, repairing muscle tissues, and reducing inflammation. This strategic intake of nutrients aids in faster recovery, prepares your body for future workouts, and minimizes muscle soreness. It's not just about consuming calories; it's about choosing the right types of nutrients at the right time to optimize recovery.

The concept of the anabolic window, the period immediately after your workout during which your body is most receptive to nutrient uptake, is crucial for optimal recovery. This window, typically considered to last between thirty minutes to two hours post-exercise, is when your muscles are primed to absorb glucose to replenish glycogen stores and amino acids to aid in protein synthesis. Missing this window can slow down your recovery process, potentially leading to prolonged soreness and fatigue. Therefore, timing your nutrient intake to fall within this window can significantly enhance your recovery speed and efficiency.

Foods that combine proteins and carbohydrates are ideal during this period. Carbohydrates help replenish the glycogen that has been depleted during your workout, while proteins provide the amino acids necessary for muscle repair and growth. A ratio of about 3:1 carbohydrates to protein is often recommended for endurance athletes, while those focusing on strength training might benefit from a ratio closer to 2:1. It's also beneficial to include some healthy fats in your recovery meal, though in smaller quantities since fats can slow the digestion process.

A practical example of a balanced post-workout meal could be a smoothie made with bananas, a scoop of protein powder, a handful of spinach, and a tablespoon of peanut butter. This combination provides a quick, easily digestible blend of proteins and carbohydrates, plus the added benefit of micronutrients from the spinach. Another good option is a turkey and avocado wrap made from whole grains. This offers a solid mix of proteins, carbs, and healthy fats. These meals address your immediate nutritional needs and also support your long-term health and training goals.

For athletes with hectic schedules, ensuring proper post-workout nutrition can be challenging, especially when access to whole foods is limited. In such cases, planning ahead is key. Portable, nutrient-rich snacks can be a lifesaver. Consider packing homemade energy bars, a mix of nuts and dried fruit, or a pre-prepared high-protein sandwich. These options are convenient and also provide the necessary nutrients to kickstart your recovery process. You can also keep a protein shake or a carbohydrate-rich sports drink in your bag to provide a quick and effective way to meet your nutrition needs until you can have a full meal.

The importance of this nutritional strategy cannot be overstated. By prioritizing your post-workout nutrition, you not only enhance your recovery and performance but also lay the groundwork for a stronger, more resilient body. It's a simple yet powerful way to ensure that each workout contributes positively to your athletic goals, helping you to maintain consistency and progress in your training. As you continue to develop and refine your post-workout nutrition plan, remember that what you feed your body after a workout is just as important as the training itself. This understanding will guide you in making informed choices that support both your immediate recovery and your long-term athletic development, keeping you on track toward achieving your highest potential in your chosen sport.

7.5 Managing Nutrition on Limited Budgets and Resources

Navigating the landscape of maintaining a nutritious diet while managing a tight budget can often feel like a challenging balancing act, especially for teen athletes whose dietary needs are crucial for their performance and overall development. However, eating well doesn't have to break the bank. With smart shopping strategies and an emphasis on cost-effectiveness, you can fuel your athletic endeavors without straining your wallet.

The cornerstone of budget-friendly nutrition is planning. Start by planning your meals for the week ahead. This approach saves money by reducing impulse purchases and ensures that you consume a balanced diet throughout the week. When you go shopping, stick to your list to avoid buying unnecessary items. Bulk buying can also be economical, especially for staples like rice, beans, and pasta, which have long shelf lives and form the basis of numerous nutritious meals. Additionally, consider shopping at local farmers' markets near the end of the day when sellers are more likely to offer discounts on fresh produce to avoid taking it back home.

Another effective strategy is to focus on seasonal produce. Fruits and vegetables that are in season are not only cheaper but also at their nutritional peak. Incorporating these into your diet can provide both variety and optimal nutrients. Frozen fruits and vegetables can be a great alternative, as they are often less expensive than their fresh counterparts and are frozen at the peak of their ripeness, which preserves their nutritional value. These options are particularly useful for smoothies or as additions to oatmeal and yogurts, providing a quick and nutritious boost to your meals.

Cooking at home is significantly less expensive and healthier than eating out. It gives you full control over what goes into your food, allowing you to make healthy choices and watch your portion sizes. Preparing large batches of meals that can be refrigerated or frozen in individual portions can save both time and money. Dishes like stews, casseroles, and stir-fries give you the opportunity to incorporate a variety of nutrient-dense foods and are generally inexpensive to make.

Understanding which foods give you the most nutritional bang for your buck is crucial. Foods like eggs, canned tuna, legumes, oatmeal, and whole-grain bread are affordable and packed with nutrients essential for athletic performance. Eggs, for instance, are an excellent source of protein and contain vitamins and minerals crucial for recovery and muscle development. Legumes, such as beans and lentils, are not only cheap but are also high in fiber and protein, making them an excellent meat substitute for athletes on a budget.

Access to adequate nutrition should ideally be a right, not a privilege. However, disparities exist, and sometimes, even the best budgeting isn't enough to meet all your nutritional needs. It's important to know that there are resources available to help. Many communities have programs that provide access to affordable or free nutritious food. School programs, local food banks, and community gardens are valuable resources that can provide assistance. Additionally, some organizations are dedicated to helping athletes meet their nutritional needs. Exploring these options can provide you with the support necessary to maintain your diet and performance.

Incorporating these strategies into your daily life will help you manage your nutrition on a budget, but, just as importantly, they will also teach you valuable life skills in budget management and nutritional planning. By being mindful of how you spend and what you eat, you ensure that every meal is a step toward reaching your peak athletic performance.

As we close this chapter on nutrition, remember that your journey toward peak performance is fueled by more than just physical training. Nutrition and hydration play pivotal roles in how you perform and recover. The strategies outlined here are designed to help you navigate the complexities of nutritional planning, ensuring that you have the energy and nutrients needed to succeed. As you move forward, carry with you the knowledge that proper nutrition is within reach, regardless of budget constraints, and is essential for your growth and success as an athlete.

Chapter 8

Setting the Stage for Long-Term Athletic Success

Now that you've seen how looking backward at the lessons you learned during the pandemic can help you to achieve success in the future, it's time to look at how you can achieve long-term athletic success. Embarking on the journey from high school to college athletics is like stepping onto a larger stage, one that promises new challenges and grander rewards. This transition isn't just about scaling up in competition; it's a pivotal period that shapes your athletic career and personal growth. In order to stand at this threshold, armed with your talent and dreams, planning your path meticulously becomes crucial. This planning involves enhancing your athletic prowess and also strategically navigating the academic demands and financial aspects of college sports. This chapter will provide you with a guide through this intricate process, ensuring you're as prepared off the field as you are on it.

8.1 From High School to College Athletics: Planning Your Path

Mapping the Transition

Transitioning from high school to college athletics requires more than just a physical readiness; it demands a mental and strategic preparation. First, understand that the level of competition is about to intensify, and so should your training. College athletes are often the best from their high schools, which means every teammate and opponent is likely as talented and driven as you are, if not more. Preparing for this requires a shift in your training regimen, possibly increasing your training hours and incorporating more strength and conditioning work.

Academically, the rigors will also increase. Balancing a tougher athletic schedule with more demanding academic work is a skill that needs cultivating early on. Begin by engaging with your future coaches and academic advisors to understand the expectations and support systems in place. Consider summer bridge programs that many colleges offer, which can help you adjust to the college workload before the official semester starts. These programs are invaluable in providing a smoother transition, giving you a head start in managing your time and responsibilities effectively.

Recruitment Process

Getting noticed by college scouts involves more than standout performances. Start by identifying schools that not only have strong athletic programs but also academic programs that match your interests. Once you have a list, reach out to the coaches with a well-crafted email expressing your interest and including a highlight reel of your performances. Remember, communication is key—be proactive, follow up respectfully, and show genuine interest in their programs.

Attending sports camps and showcases can significantly boost your visibility. These events are often teeming with scouts looking for the next star athlete. Ensure you're in top form during these showcases by utilizing the skills and techniques we've talked about throughout this book. Every drill and game should be treated as a mini-audition. It's not just about your skills; coaches are looking for athletes who display leadership, resilience, and a strong work ethic.

Scholarships and Financial Planning

Navigating the financial aspect of college sports is a critical step. Athletic scholarships can offer substantial support, but they vary widely in terms of what they cover and how they are awarded. Division I schools typically offer more full-ride scholarships compared to Division II or III. However, competition for these scholarships is fierce. Research the schools you are interested in and understand their scholarship criteria and the process of application. It's also wise to apply for academic scholarships; they can provide additional financial support and are not contingent on your athletic performance.

Balancing Academics and Athletics

The dual demands of academics and athletics can overwhelm even the most seasoned athletes. Time management becomes your greatest ally. Utilize planners or digital apps to keep track of your training schedules, classes, and assignments. Don't hesitate to use the academic resources most colleges offer, like tutoring sessions and study groups. Communicate regularly with your professors and coaches about your schedule—they can offer flexibility during your sports seasons.

Most importantly, prioritize your health—both mental and physical. The pressures of maintaining high performance in both areas can lead to burnout if not managed properly. Ensure you are getting enough rest, eating properly, and taking time to relax and enjoy your college experience. Remember, college is not just about sports; it's a time for personal growth, exploring new interests, and making lifelong friendships. By planning carefully and embracing the comprehensive college experience, you set the stage for success both in your athletic career and beyond.

8.2 The Role of Mentorship in Athletic Development

Mentorship, often overlooked, is a powerful catalyst in both your athletic and personal development. Having a mentor can provide you with guidance, support, and insights that are invaluable in navigating the complex landscape of competitive sports. A mentor serves not just as a coach but as a trusted advisor who can share wisdom from their own experiences, helping you avoid common pitfalls and make informed decisions about your career and life. This relationship can profoundly impact your growth, offering a blend of encouragement, constructive criticism, and personal anecdotes that can inspire and motivate you.

There are many benefits to having a mentor in sports. Mentors can help you refine your techniques, but their influence extends far beyond the physical aspects of your training. They can assist you in setting realistic yet challenging goals, developing mental toughness, and maintaining motivation during tough times. Mentors also often provide emotional support, serving as a sounding board during periods of doubt or frustration. They can help you navigate the highs and lows of your athletic journey, ensuring you remain focused and resilient. Mentors can introduce you to a broader network of contacts in the sports industry as well, which can be crucial for your career advancement. This networking aspect can open doors to new opportunities, whether it's scholarships, competitive slots, or professional engagements.

Finding the right mentor involves identifying someone who not only possesses the expertise you seek but also aligns with your personality and values. Start by looking at your current sports club, school, or community sports networks. Coaches, former athletes, or even sports educators can make excellent mentors. Attend sports clinics, workshops, and seminars where you can meet and interact with potential mentors. When choosing a mentor, look for qualities such as experience, empathy, communication skills, and a genuine interest in helping others succeed. A good mentor should be someone you respect and can see yourself learning from—not just about sports but about life skills.

Being an engaged and proactive mentee is crucial to getting the most out of the mentorship experience. This involves being open to feedback, actively participating in discussions, and showing eagerness to learn and grow. Prepare for your meetings with your mentor by having specific questions or topics you want to discuss. This shows that you value their time and advice and are committed to your development. Be receptive to constructive criticism and be willing to step out of your comfort zone to implement their suggestions. Remember, the goal of mentorship is not just to affirm what you are already doing well but to challenge you to evolve and improve.

Mentorship in sports is more than just learning how to play better; it's about growing as a person and an athlete. The insights, encouragement, and real-world advice from a mentor can be pivotal in helping you navigate your athletic career and life. By actively seeking out mentorship opportunities, engaging fully in the process, and choosing mentors who truly align with your aspirations and values, you set yourself on a path to not just immediate success but long-term satisfaction and growth in your sports career and beyond.

8.3 Navigating Sponsorships and Media as a Young Athlete

Navigating the world of sponsorships and media as a young athlete can feel like stepping onto a new playing field where the rules aren't quite as clear as the lines on a track or the boundaries of a field. Understanding how sponsorships work is your first step. Essentially, sponsorships are partnerships where a brand aligns itself with you because they believe your athletic persona and achievements can help promote their products or services. There are various types of sponsorships, ranging from gear and clothing—which are often product-based—to financial backing for training and competitions. What sponsors are looking for can vary widely, but primarily, they are attracted to athletes who not only excel in their sports but also carry a positive image that reflects well on the brand. This means that your performance in your sport is as crucial as how you present yourself publicly and online.

Handling media attention is another critical aspect of your career that requires savvy and preparation. As your profile rises, so does the interest from various media outlets, including social media platforms, sports blogs, local news, and more. Managing this attention starts with proper media training, which can help you understand how to interact with journalists, handle interviews, and present yourself in a manner that best represents both you and your sport. Training might cover how to answer tricky questions, maintaining your poise when faced with unexpected situations, and the importance of staying true to your message. Remember, every interview and public appearance is an opportunity to enhance your personal brand or could potentially harm it if not handled correctly.

Personal branding is about how you market yourself as an athlete and a public figure. It encompasses everything from your social media profiles to how you conduct yourself in public and interact with fans and media. Building and maintaining a positive personal brand requires consistency, authenticity, and strategic planning. Your brand should reflect who you are as an athlete and a person, showcasing your strengths, passions, and values. This can attract more sponsorship opportunities and increase your visibility in the sports world. It's important to stay active and engaged in the right way on social media platforms, using it to share your training progress, achievements, and even setbacks. This kind of transparency builds trust and relatability with your audience.

Lastly, understanding the legal and ethical considerations in sponsorships and media relations is crucial. This includes knowing the details of any contract you sign, from what you are required to do to how long the contract lasts and what compensation you will receive. Always have contracts reviewed by a professional to ensure your rights are protected and you fully understand your obligations. Ethically, it's vital to only partner with brands and products you genuinely like or use, as insincerity can be easily spotted by your audience and can damage your credibility. Several years ago, a middle school principal shared an issue that he came across while looking at two applicants for an open teaching position at his school. While reviewing their references and social media, he saw some things that immediately caused him to dismiss them from moving forward to the interview stage. Why was that? They had posted content that showed them involved in activities that were not conducive to what a school would want in a teacher. The lesson here is to be aware of the implications of your online behavior—what you share on social media can have a lasting impact on your personal brand, relationships with sponsors, and in your career.

Navigating this complex landscape can initially seem daunting, but with the right knowledge and preparation, you can manage sponsorships and media attention in a way that benefits your career and upholds the integrity of your sporting journey. As you grow in your athletic career, these elements will become integral parts of your professional life, influencing not just your sports performance but also your marketability and public persona. Whether you are just starting to attract media attention or are managing multiple sponsorships, remember that how you handle these aspects can have a significant impact on your future opportunities and success in sports.

8.4 Anticipating and Adapting to Future Challenges in Sports

As athletes, your journey is one of constant evolution—not only in your physical capabilities but also in adapting to the shifting landscapes of sports. The fields, courts, and tracks you compete on today are not what they will be tomorrow.

Looking beyond the track, field, or court, it's essential to consider life after sports. While the thrill of competition is unmatched, building a life outside of athletics is crucial. Start by exploring educational opportunities that can pave the way for alternative careers. Many athletes turn to coaching, sports management, or entrepreneurial ventures that keep them connected to the sports world. Others find rewarding careers in entirely different fields, using the discipline and leadership skills they've honed in sports to excel in business, arts, or community service. Preparing for this transition involves networking, continuing education, and sometimes, internships that provide a taste of potential career paths.

Building a legacy in sports is about more than records and championships; it's about the impact you leave on your community and future generations. Those that successfully do so have overcome what I refer to as one of the twin cancers of any team, selfishness and laziness. Always remember, the platform you have as a participant, coach, business person, etc. is a privilege. Standing on that platform as a positive role model for future young people will help to set a high bar so they too can reach their full potential.

Engaging in community service, advocating for causes you're passionate about, and mentoring young athletes are ways to extend your influence beyond your athletic achievements. These activities not only enrich your life and others' but also solidify your role as a leader and role model. Whether it's setting up sports clinics, volunteering in local community centers, or starting a nonprofit, your legacy can be a beacon that lights the way for those coming up behind you.

Looking ahead, the future of sports is as exciting as it is uncertain. By staying adaptable, educated, and engaged, you ensure that your career—both during and after your athletic prime—is as rewarding as possible. Embrace the changes, plan for the future, and build a legacy that lasts. This proactive approach will prepare you for the transitions ahead and also ensures that your career in sports is just the beginning of a long and fulfilling journey.

As we close this chapter, take a moment to reflect on the importance of forward-thinking in your athletic career. The landscape of sports will continue to evolve, presenting new challenges and opportunities. By staying informed about emerging trends, embracing adaptability, planning for life after sports, and aiming to leave a lasting impact, you equip yourself for success in all facets of life.

Looking ahead, the next chapter will explore how embracing community and cultural engagement can further enrich your athletic journey and personal growth, setting the stage for a well-rounded and impactful career.

Chapter 9

Beyond the Game: Life Skills from Sports

As you stand on the precipice of this new chapter, it's vital to recognize that the skills honed on the field don't just win games—they can transform lives. Within this chapter, we dive into how the discipline of sports can sculpt not only a seasoned athlete but also a formidable leader in everyday life. The agility to dodge a tackle, the resilience to rise from a fall, and the foresight to pass the ball at just the right moment are great tactics and important life lessons in disguise. Here, we explore the profound impact of sports beyond the scoreboard, where the true victory lies in the invaluable life skills you carry into the world.

9.1 LEADERSHIP AND TEAMWORK: LESSONS FROM THE FIELD

Transferring Skills to Everyday Life

The skills you cultivate as an athlete—leadership, teamwork, communication—are not confined to the boundaries of your sport. They spill over into every area of your life, providing a foundation for success beyond the game. Consider leadership, often seen as the ability to guide and inspire a team toward a common goal. This skill is equally applicable in a classroom setting, where you might lead a group project or a study session. It teaches you how to motivate peers, delegate tasks based on individual strengths, and make strategic decisions—skills that are invaluable in any professional environment.

Teamwork, too, translates seamlessly into everyday situations. Sports teach you to recognize the value of diverse skills and personalities, understanding that a team's strength lies in its collective capability. This lesson is vital in the workplace, where collaborative projects require you to work harmoniously with colleagues who bring different perspectives and skills to the table. By applying the principles of effective teamwork learned in sports, you can enhance productivity and foster a positive work environment, proving that the whole truly is greater than the sum of its parts.

Building Effective Teams

The art of building an effective team extends beyond knowing each player's physical capabilities—it's about understanding personalities, identifying how different members complement each other, and fostering a sense of mutual respect. These principles are directly applicable to forming groups in academic or professional settings. For instance, when tasked with a group project, you can utilize your understanding of team dynamics to allocate roles that align with each member's strengths, just as a captain might position players on the field. This strategic placement can lead to more efficient project completion and a more harmonious group dynamic.

Leadership Opportunities

Sports offer numerous opportunities to develop leadership skills, from captaining a team to leading by example through dedication and work ethic. These experiences prepare you for leadership roles in other areas of your life. For example, the confidence and assertive communication required to lead a team on the field can empower you to take on leadership roles in school clubs or community groups. The ability to make quick, strategic decisions under pressure is a trait that employers highly value, positioning you as a strong candidate for managerial roles in your future career.remember that the discipline, leadership, and teamwork you cultivate through sports are more than just strategies for winning games. They are tools that empower you to lead, inspire, and succeed in every arena of life. By embracing these lessons and applying them beyond the sports field, you set yourself up for a fulfilling and impactful life, marked by achievements that extend far beyond athletic accomplishments.

9.2 Time Management and Discipline: the Athlete's Advantage

Mastering the clock—both on and off the field—is a skill that you, as an athlete, have been cultivating, perhaps even without realizing its profound impact on every facet of your life. The rigorous schedule of practices, games, and competitions teaches you to manage your time efficiently, ensuring that every minute counts. This ability to juggle various commitments extends far beyond the sports arena into your academic and personal life, providing a framework that can help you achieve a balance that many struggle to find.

Effective time management begins with prioritization. As an athlete, you learn early on to identify which tasks require immediate attention and which can be scheduled for later. This skill is invaluable in academic settings where deadlines are as relentless as game schedules. Utilizing tools like planners or digital apps to keep track of assignments, exams, and training sessions can help you visualize your week, allocate time effectively, and avoid last-minute rushes. Setting specific times for study, just as you set specific times for training, can help in maintaining a consistent routine, making it easier to manage your workload and reduce stress. Moreover, learning to say no to activities that do not align with your goals is crucial. Just as you might decline a late-night outing before a game day, being selective about social engagements around crucial academic deadlines is essential for maintaining focus and achieving academic success.

Discipline is the backbone of effective time management. In sports, discipline translates into showing up for practice on time, adhering to a training regimen, and following a nutrition plan—all critical for peak performance. Similarly, in your academic and personal life, discipline involves setting and sticking to your study routines, ensuring you get adequate rest, and managing your social and family time efficiently. The key is consistency. Just as sporadic training won't make you a better athlete, inconsistent studying won't lead to good grades. Establishing and maintaining a routine that balances all aspects of your life can foster a sense of security and control, which as we learned from the pandemic is especially valuable in high-pressure periods.

Balancing your commitments effectively requires an understanding of your limits. Overcommitting can lead to burnout, a state all too familiar in both sports and academics. Recognize the signs of fatigue—whether it's physical tiredness from training or mental exhaustion from studying—and give yourself permission to take breaks. Effective time management isn't about cramming as many tasks into your day as possible; it's about optimizing your energy and maintaining your health so you can perform well in all areas. Scheduled breaks, relaxation periods, and leisure activities are essential components of a well-rounded schedule. They provide not only rest but also rejuvenation, allowing you to return to your tasks with renewed energy and focus.As you navigate through your daily activities, remember that the skills you develop on the field are powerful tools that can help you achieve your academic and personal goals. Time management and discipline are among the most significant of these skills, providing a foundation for success that extends well beyond sports. By continuing to apply these skills across all areas of your life, you are setting yourself up for a balanced, productive, and fulfilling journey, no matter where your passions and pursuits may lead you.

9.3 Resilience in Life: Applying Athletic Mental Toughness to Everyday Challenges

Resilience might first manifest on the field or court, where you push through a tough game or recover from a hard fall, but its true value becomes apparent in the broader context of life's challenges. The mental toughness developed through sports equips you with a unique set of skills that are incredibly effective when faced with life's inevitable obstacles. Each setback in sports, whether it's missing a crucial shot or losing a significant match, trains you to handle disappointment and to channel these feelings into a drive for improvement. This same resilience is invaluable when you encounter academic challenges, personal setbacks, or professional obstacles.

For instance, the resilience learned from coming back from a sports injury with patience and determination can teach you how to navigate personal hardships, such as recovering from a setback in school like a poor exam score. Instead of letting it define or discourage you, you can use it as an opportunity to evaluate your study methods, seek additional help, or develop a more effective preparation strategy. Just as in sports, where reviewing game footage can provide insights for future performances, academic and life challenges can be approached with a mindset geared toward learning and growth.

Sports also teach effective coping mechanisms that are highly applicable to other life areas. Techniques such as visualization, deep breathing, and setting small, manageable goals can help manage the stress of a looming college application deadline or a job interview. Sports teach you that rest and recovery are as vital as persistent effort, a principle that can help maintain your mental health during particularly stressful times. Learning to recognize when to push through and when to step back and recuperate can help you manage your energy and keep stress levels in check, preventing burnout.

Encouraging a growth mindset is another crucial takeaway from the world of sports. This mindset, centered on the belief that abilities and intelligence can be developed through dedication and hard work, is directly transferable to virtually every aspect of life. In sports, a growth mindset might lead you to view a loss as a learning opportunity rather than a failure. Similarly, in academic or professional settings, challenges can be seen as chances to grow and learn rather than insurmountable obstacles. Cultivating this mindset can foster resilience by helping you to persist in the face of challenges, stay motivated, and continually seek ways to improve yourself.

As we wrap up this exploration of how resilience in sports translates to broader life skills, remember that the qualities that make you a strong athlete also prepare you for the challenges outside the athletic arena. The discipline, mental toughness, and capacity to learn from setbacks are tools that will serve you well in any context, helping you to navigate the complexities of life with confidence and determination.

Inspirational Stories

This last section of the book provides examples of students I have coached who have grown in the principles of mental toughness. I think you will find them inspiring and useful for your own journey.

Lauren Edgar, Northeastern Tennis, class of 2024, valedictorian

It was the final match of my senior year, and after an incredible season, I was pushing myself to end on a win. The match started off well. I was thriving under my own pressure, hitting shots with depth, angle, and speed. I exuded mental strength through my body language. The first set was mine to claim, 6-0.

I went into the second set confident, not yet knowing the mental toughness I would soon need to practice. It immediately started out tougher. My opponent took a few games early on, wearing down my morale. Since talking to her coach, she had altered her tactics to prevent me from winning rallies with angled shots, the skill in which I felt the most confident. I felt my mental toughness deteriorate as she won point after point. Instead of adapting my own strategy, I let my negative thoughts bring me down. I soon experienced difficulty breathing and a racing heart rate while standing in place to serve. Eventually, I decided to leave the court, preventing my anxiety attack from escalating further. I sat between my mom and my coach. They tried to cheer me up, but when I returned to the court, I still struggled.

I lost the second set. I suddenly became grateful for the sun beating down on the tennis courts because it meant that I was given a choice: continue the match in a third set, or a much shorter tiebreak. (Coach's note: in our tennis league, if the match has been decided, the athletes that are still playing will do a ten-point tiebreaker.)

During the pause between sets, my coach asked me what I wanted to do. Given my emotional state, I didn't want to keep playing, but I also didn't want everyone to see me quit. I considered my options. A third set would give me more time to think. But, is that what would benefit me when overthinking was what had brought me down in the first place? Meanwhile, a tiebreak would create stress for both my opponent and me, but did I really want any more stress right now?

With ideas swarming my mind, I compared my performance in the first and second sets. Both sets were equally taxing. The difference, I realized, was my approach. In the second set, I had stopped fighting back when my opponent challenged me. If I wanted to win this match, I needed to turn the tables and return the pressure to my opponent. So, I chose the tiebreak.

Ultimately, I won the match. It served as a lesson in using mental toughness to my advantage. When obstacles arise, I must remind myself that I can thrive under pressure.

Fred Mulbah, Basketball Player

Even after teaching at several schools in multiple states, basketball high flier Fred Mulbah is the finest overall high school athlete I have ever seen. I first met him at Northeastern High School, where he always played before huge crowds that packed the gyms to see his incredible skills. He then pursued basketball at Pitt Johnstown and set many additional scoring and assist records there before finally going to play professionally in the European League in Portugal.

Better yet, Fred is an outstanding person and role model for the youth he serves with his basketball coaching. Fred has a Youtube channel under his name, which I encourage you to check out, especially the video of his highlight reel.

Hayden Dallam, Class of 2024, Northeastern High School

For me, mental toughness is all about being within myself and not worrying about events I cannot control in the world around me. There was one tennis match where the first two sets went 3-6, 6-3, so the third set was big and I had to stay 100 percent locked in. The match went to 6-6, and we went into a tiebreaker. I made sure to stay focused and not be distracted by the crowd, the shots the other player was hitting, or any other outside influences.

One of the biggest strategies that helped me to tune out distractions was keeping my eyes down for most of the time in between points. I also made sure to take a few seconds to myself before each serve to prepare and get my head right for the next point. I practiced positive thinking, telling myself to be loose and just swing and play because when I make things more complicated than they are, I start having problems.

I also have to make sure to not take the game too seriously, but rather just go out and have fun. There were a few matches this season where I put so much pressure on myself and lost to some really bad players. I was very stiff and not enjoying myself at all, and this only led to one bad shot after another. When I make it serious by putting pressure and expectations on myself, I give myself no chance to play freely and hit some shots.

To counteract this when I'm playing I mess around a little, celebrating points or being goofy because if I'm not enjoying it, then I'm not engaged and I'm not ready to go when me or my team need it. Also, having a good time helps me to tune out the distractions because I'm enjoying what I'm doing.

All in all, mental toughness for me is being fully focused and into what I'm doing. There are many ways of going about that, and I have found the ways that are most impactful for me to help me be my best.

Randall Diabe, 197 lbs. Competitor at Appalachian State College

When it comes to mental toughness in wrestling, I always told myself, "Expect it to be hard; then accept it." Another favorite is, "Believe in yourself so much that other people think you're delusional."

(Coach's note: I witnessed this attitude in Randall while coaching him.)

Randall Diabe, Assistant Coach at Appalachian State coaching Tomas Brooker

Jeb Payne, Northeastern High School

A Story from My Wrestling Career:

I was the top seed at the Governor Mifflin Tournament when I found myself in the quarter finals against a kid from New Jersey, the #8 seed. I felt very good going into that match having scored a first period pin in the round of sixteen. During this match I found myself facing a much tougher opponent than I had expected of the #8 seed. Late in the third period I was down by three points, and we were in the neutral position. With time running out, I knew that if I had any hope of winning the match, I needed to take him down to his back to score the take down and back points. Scoring only a takedown would not get me the victory.

My father (and coach) was telling me to attempt a throw that my club coach had shown me over the summer. It was a move that I had hit a few times in practice but I had never been in a situation to hit it in a match. To this day, I don't know if it even has a name, but with less than thirty seconds on the clock, I secured the Russian Tie, transitioned into a High Russian, and from there I hit the Lat Throw. I secured two points for the takedown and three back points, securing me the victory as time ran out.

The kid from New Jersey, we later found out, was much better than the #8 seed and went on to dominate his way to third place in that competition, doing well at other tournaments that year, too.

In that fight, I was facing an upset with only a short time remaining, but I knew I had to stay composed and never give up in order to overcome the obstacle. This memory has always been a reminder that while at practice you should drill the basics over and over but also make sure you drill new moves because you never know when you will need them. It's better to try them for the first time in the practice room than on the mat.

Jeb Payne, Present Day

A Story from My Coaching Career:

The 2024 wrestling season was my first year taking over the junior high program where I wrestled as a kid. The season was going incredibly well, and we were heading into the tournament with a 6-1 dual record on the year. But weather conditions caused the tournament to be rescheduled to a new weekend. Because we originally thought we wouldn't be competing or practicing the weekend it was rescheduled to, two of our highest scoring starters were not able to attend the tournament due to prior commitments that weekend. On top of that we had two other starters out sick and another coming off an injury, being cleared to wrestle but still not looking 100 percent.

The odds were not looking good for us. We would be arriving with only a partial lineup, and two of the teams we would be up against, we had just narrowly beat earlier in the year, while another team out of Lancaster, PA, was known to be really tough to beat.

Going into the tournament I preached to the kids that they needed to stay mentally tough. In order to fill the lineup, some of them were going to be bumped around, meaning they would wrestle in different weight classes than they were used to. During our first match with one of the teams that we narrowly beat earlier in the year, we bumped up our 130, 138, 145, and 155 pounders. We came away from that match with a backup pulling off a big victory and our wrestler who moved to 155 pulling off a crucial overtime victory.

The tournament was coming down to one of the last matches that I knew would make or break the dual meet. It was our 170-pound wrestler; the one who was coming off an injury. Earlier in the year he got pinned by this opponent, but this day would be different. He proved how mentally tough he was by wrestling his heart out and only losing by decision despite still being slowed down by injury. He only gave up three team points instead of six, helping us secure the team win 34 to 33. This is a great example of how even in a loss you can benefit the team by staying mentally tough and never giving up.

Alexander C. Jones, United States Naval Officer

This is a story of perseverance. One key point to note is that obstacles are great moments of mental clarity because they are real. They're real moments of real accountability and real direction. We as people face some of our most defining moments, not as adults, but as teenagers. Young aspiring people that are on the cusp of our own greatness.

From a young age, my dream of joining the Navy was a constant beacon, guiding me through the tumultuous waves of adolescence. High school brought both triumphs and trials—excelling in sports and social circles, yet often finding trouble. As a rambunctious teenager with grand aspirations, discipline was a hard-earned lesson. My path took a dark turn at age sixteen, when a felony charge threatened to extinguish my dreams and aspirations. A year later, two misdemeanors for underage drinking seemed to seal the fate of my military aspirations.

However, my wise grandmother's advice sparked a transformation. She said, "Everything that happens to you and for you is part of your story. You can let that story end here… or begin here." This wisdom was cherished, turning obstacles into testimonies and releasing rigid expectations of the future. The focus shifted to hard work and the belief that it would lead to a beautiful destination. After my high school graduation, the pursuit of my military dream continued while delivering pizzas for Domino's Pizza. Despite being denied twice by the Navy and enrolling at North Carolina Central University, the quest for stability and a military career never wavered.

The journey was arduous, with rejections from every branch of service, including two denials from the Marine Corps. But perseverance paid off, and the opportunity to join the Marines finally arrived. Once in, the ambition to succeed opened doors to numerous opportunities. I was able to use my background in professional hospitality to join the military culinary program within the first year. A phenomenal career began to unfold as I made history by being the first junior level Marine, E-3 Lance Corporal, to be admitted into the prestigious Marine Aide Culinary Program. Opportunities arrived to serve in the Pentagon for the highest-ranked military executive level officers and even the presidential level of leadership within the government, a testament to my hard work and determination.

Alexander Jones with his amazing wife, Shaneka.

Today, blessed with a divine calling, my journey continues as a naval officer and a chaplain, pursuing a Master of Divinity from Duke University. This is a story of resilience, perseverance, and faith, a testament to the power of never giving up on one's dreams.

To any teen reading this story, you yourself are immensely extraordinary. There is something about you that will not let you give up on your dreams. That something is your legacy reminding you that there's still work to be done, still more effort to give. There is a part inside each of us that can encourage us that our dreams are better off deferred. I had so many times where I questioned my own ambitions, mainly because they didn't look like everyone else's. That is and what always will be what makes you special; that's the extraordinary part of you that says "keep going."

So, I encourage you to go a little further toward your goals. Step a little bit further away from your own comforts. I promise that your own ambitions will surprise you in just how far you will go.

Chris Gross, Deposit-Hancock Baseball

Building my mental toughness was not an overnight process. There is no magic bullet to becoming mentally tough, but there are steps you can take to work in the right direction. Shooting to become a master of discipline, persistence, and self-awareness is an absolute necessity in becoming mentally tough. You need to be disciplined enough to work, even when you aren't motivated. Persistent enough to "stay the course," so to speak, regardless of shortcomings and failures. Self-aware enough to know that "I can." These traits are not easy to build into your personality but it can be done through various methods of enduring the "suck," utilizing meditation and training your thoughts to have an outside-looking perspective to help with your endurance. Also, always have a "why not me" mentality. Learn to embrace the hard things, learn to love the work, and learn an "I can" mindset.

Pressure is as big as *you* make it. How you perceive the external is synonymous with the impact it will have internally. As soon as you have conquered that, you no longer have to be someone who feels the pressure, but you can be someone that applies pressure.

Kevin Crane

When I started my senior year at Hancock Central School, Hancock, NY, I played football for my school as a running back. Although I wasn't very big, I was pretty quick and could take a good hit. During a game against a team from Oxford, PA, my life changed forever.

On one particular play, the quarterback handed me the ball and I attempted to run the play up the middle as designed. Unfortunately for me, a defensive linebacker hit me straight on and I landed hard on the field, resulting in my right shoulder becoming dislocated. Coach Walt Smith immediately came out on the field, felt my shoulder as I lay on the ground, and gently scooped me up to walk me back to the sideline. The pain I felt from that injury was a pain like no other. I was quickly taken by ambulance to the local hospital where the doctors eventually put my shoulder back in place. That was the end of my football days, and that injury caused me many difficulties and pain for years to come.

My main love of sports was practicing martial arts. I had actually started my martial arts journey at the age of sixteen and continued working out on my own through my senior year of high school. Tim, who was our school wrestling coach, was kind enough to allow me to hang a kicking bag in the wrestling room of our school so I could practice.

After graduation I attended Penn State University and became the president of the newly formed Karate Club. That first year I participated in a local karate tournament held at Villanova University, just for the chance to do some fighting competition. I beat my first opponent and, unfortunately, dislocated my shoulder again while fighting my second opponent. Off to the hospital I went to endure another round of immense pain as the doctors put my shoulder back into place. I'll spare you the details of how they do it, the length of time it takes, and the sickening feeling of the pain even while under anesthesia.

But despite this, my martial arts journey always continued. While working out at several karate venues, I ended up dislocating my shoulder about ten times in total. Each time it happened it set me back from earning my Black Belt which, at the time, was my ultimate goal. It was so frustrating and discouraging knowing this lifelong injury was never going away that there were times when I contemplated quitting martial arts. My choice came down to knowing that I would either feel the pain of defeat if I never earned my Black Belt or I would feel the pain of future injury while at least attempting to get that Black Belt. One day the answer became clear, and I will explain why.

The style of martial arts I practiced was Tang Soo Do, a Korean karate extremely similar to Taekwondo and the same karate taught by Chuck

Norris. Aside from the physical skills and attributes of Tang Soo Do, we were also taught the seven tenants of the art as follows:

- integrity,
- concentration,
- perseverance,
- respect and obedience,
- self-control,
- humility, and
- indomitable spirit.

When I made the choice to go after the Black Belt, despite knowing it would most likely lead to more dislocations of my shoulder, I decided that I needed to focus on perseverance and indomitable spirit to get me through those times. Doubt would arise when my dislocated shoulder would physically and mentally hold me back, and in those times, it would have been easier to quit and never have to go to the hospital again, but I didn't want to live with the regret of not achieving my goal. By following my heart, enduring any hardship that I faced, and maintaining a mentally tough and positive attitude, I eventually earned my 1st Degree Black Belt after twenty years!

As the years progressed, I became a PA State AAU Fighting Champion, was a co-founder of a Tang Soo Do school, taught thousands of children and adults, became an AAU coach and referee, was certified as an anti-child abductor instructor, and achieved the rank of 3rd Degree Black Belt. If I had not decided to follow the mental fundamentals of what martial arts and Tim Law were teaching, my life would not be what it is today. I am happy and fulfilled knowing that not only did I achieve my goals and dreams, but that being mentally tough has allowed me to help so many others achieve theirs, too!

Conclusion

As we draw this guide to a close, it's essential to revisit the core mission of this journey we've embarked on together: to reignite the work ethic and fitness of teen athletes in a world reshaped by the challenges of COVID-19. This book has been crafted not just as a response to a global health crisis but as a comprehensive blueprint designed to empower you as a young athlete. We've delved into strategies that aim to boost your fitness, rebuild your stamina, and elevate your performance to peak levels, all within the feasible commitment of just 40 minutes per day.

Throughout these pages, we've covered a spectrum of crucial topics—from adapting training routines to enhancing mental toughness and onto exploring the profound connection between mind and body. We've introduced practical, actionable strategies complemented by motivational stories and the latest research, tailored specifically for your unique needs during these post-COVID-19 times. The essence of our discussions aimed to equip you with the tools not only to return to your pre-pandemic performance levels but to exceed them, embracing innovations and new approaches to training and well-being.

The key takeaways from our journey together encompass stress resilience, adaptability, and a proactive stance toward personal health and fitness. These themes are interwoven with the recognition that the landscape of teen athletics has transformed, necessitating a fresh perspective on training, mental health, and community engagement in sports. By acknowledging your specific challenges and meeting them with empathy, understanding, and evidence-based solutions, this book serves as both a beacon of inspiration and a practical manual that addresses the real worries and obstacles you have faced in the recent times of uncertainty.

Now, as you turn the final pages, I encourage you to take these lessons beyond the book. Apply these strategies in your training and daily life, share them with teammates, and discuss them with coaches. There's a whole community out there that can benefit from a collective uplift in spirit and capability.

Reflecting on the journey of writing this book, my passion for supporting your growth and success in these challenging times has only deepened. Each chapter was penned with the hope that it would resonate with you, not just as athletes but as individuals facing a rapidly changing world. This guide is my heartfelt effort to contribute positively to your athletic and personal development.

Thank you sincerely for joining me on this significant journey. Your resilience and dedication in pushing through barriers, whether on the track, in the field, or in life, continue to inspire. Remember, the path to peak performance is paved with mental toughness, self-discipline, personal power, focused attention, and other important characteristics that will give them both wings and roots. Keep striving, keep pushing, and embrace each challenge as an opportunity to grow stronger and more capable.

Here's to achieving your highest potential, breaking new grounds, and setting new personal bests. Go out there and make every minute of your training count. You have the power to redefine your limits and achieve greatness.

To end, here is a very useful postscript from Alan Weis from his Monday morning memo. It will help you to further connect many successful patterns that can and will work for all of us.

How to Escape Misery

How to escape misery. That's right. I'm going to help you very quickly, very rapidly escape misery. So listen, if one or more of these apply to you, here's how you escape.

Number 1, stop internalizing and personalizing everybody else's problems. There's a word for that and it's called "neuroses." Other people have problems and they are responsible for solving them. Believing that you are somehow the one who has to take on the burden is ridiculous. Let them have the responsibility. By all means, support them. But don't think it's your internal problem or challenge to do so.

Next, forgive yourself. That's right, you deserve to be happy. Start giving yourself a break. You forgive others, right? Why not forgive yourself? The person we least forgive is the person in the mirror. So stop suffering, stop holding long and deep grudges, stop treating yourself like you ought to be beaten down. You're not unworthy. So stop telling yourself you are.

Next, stop isolating yourself. Don't avoid contact. You need a support system. It might be loved ones. It might be family. It might be friends. It might be colleagues. It might be people at work or people at clients or people in trade associations or people in the community or people at the coffee shop. Don't allow yourself to be isolated. Don't reject help that's offered. I'm not talking about unsolicited feedback. I am talking about honest-to-goodness offers of support.

Next, stop trying to please everybody. We spend a whole lot of time trying to make sure everybody else is pleased with us. Don't compromise your standards. It's okay if some people are pissed off. "What did he say?" Yes, I said it. It's all right. Your personal value doesn't depend on acceptance of others. Your personal value depends upon self-mastery. That is, how do you feel about yourself?

Next, stop comparing yourself to others. You're your own person. So, speaking of self-mastery, be ipsative not normative. In other words, who are you according to you? Stop looking at others as your standard.

Stop looking at another as the person who is your avatar. A lot of those people have feet of clay. A lot of those people are before Congressional hearings right now or they're indicted for fraud. Please stop worrying about it and just be yourself.

Next, live for the moment. Don't look back in nostalgia and don't look forward in anticipation, look around and enjoy yourself. Today is today; it won't come again. Nor will this minute. And so, enjoy yourself in the moment. That's what self-actualization is all about. Don't be afraid to relish where you are right now. Don't feel guilty about that. Enjoy yourself. Connect with that, don't dwell on past mistakes and failures. I've got news for you, you can't undo them. In fact, the best thing you can do is learn from them. But then, move on. Stop focusing on things you can no longer change. It's astounding how many people spend time focussed on things they have no power in the world to change. Making yourself miserable doesn't help others you've made miserable in the past, trust me.

Next, try to stay positive and oriented towards solutions and new levels of performance. Don't be negative. Don't always look at problems. I talk to people who sigh after every other sentence. "That's right, {sigh} well I guess I'll get more money today." Oh, that's too bad, sorry to hear it. For goodness sakes, remain positive. Self-talk is real talk. Talk to yourself positively and look at your surroundings positively. Believe me, it could be worse.

Next, don't allow yourself to be controlled by others or by circumstances. We've touched on this a little to this point. But it's too easy in a world that is trying every day to make you into something else and to fall victim to that. So don't allow yourself to be controlled. Don't worry about what the advertisements say you should be wearing. Don't worry about what unsolicited feedback tells you about your behavior or your speaking or your interactions. Don't allow yourself to be controlled by others unless you respect their opinion and unless you solicit it.

Next, take on involvement and responsibility. People who take on accountabilities are better off. The best people I meet on committees, on boards, on task forces are those who stand out in a crowd and chair something, or head something, or take a risk. Try new things. You'll be successful. You'll get increased satisfaction. But don't sit around avoiding involvement, avoiding responsibility. The world is not like that. Step out of the crowd. Get into the limelight.

Two more. First, set realistic expectations for yourself. If you want to lose weight, if you want to get in shape, fine. But telling yourself to lose thirty-five pounds in two months is ridiculous. On the other hand, signing up for a gym and promising to go three times a week is probably pretty achievable. Don't set unrealistic goals. Don't tell yourself you're going to make a million dollars one year from now. If you do, great! Listen, I'm not against having all the confidence in the world. But it's much better to say, "Someday, in the meanwhile, I'm going to double my present income from $200,000 to $400,000." So don't set unrealistic expectations. Set expectations and achievements that you're likely to hit.

Finally, base your worth on things that you believe in. Don't base your worth on externals. Not external feedback. Not the way you look. Not what you do. Not your job title. Not the possessions you have. Love yourself unconditionally. Don't base your worth on things to be pointed to. Now that comes from someone who wrote *Million Dollar Consulting*, and I am well aware of that. But I also know who I am. You have to know you're a good person. You have to believe that you're a good person. And if you do, the world will look a lot better because you are a good person.

© 2008 Alan Weiss. All rights reserved.
Monday Morning memo, "reprinted with permission."

Tim is also available for presentations to teens and schools on mental toughness, including the key "why's" of its importance for each person's future success. He can be reached by email, tlaw5111@gmail.com, or text, 717-781-4078. (Texting after sending an email will increase the chances of receiving a response in a timely manner.)

Additionally, if you are curious to locate the interviews on Tim's YouTube channel, Playing It Forward Coaching, of some of the previously mentioned people who are not named in this book, please text Tim at 717-781-4078.

Please take just a couple minutes to put in an Amazon Review comment on a mentally tough experience you may have had yourself and how you handled it.

Simply scan the QR code or visit the link below to leave your review. Your help is much appreciated.

http://www:amazon.com/review/review-your-purchase/?asin=B0DF2Z1N9P

Dedication

This book is dedicated to the most amazing, most *mentally tough* people—my parents, James and Alice Law. Raising their brood of six—myself; my brothers Steve, Tom, and Dave; and my sisters, Anne Marie and Barbara—was not an easy road, and they did a wonderful job keeping us balanced and in perspective. Their sense of humor was legendary as well!

Another huge thank you goes to my Oswego State College wrestling Coach, James Howard, who believed in this skinny college freshman and opened many doors for me on and off the mats. Thank you, Coach Howard!

Lastly, this dedication wouldn't be complete without thanking one more man who was a true key in my teaching and coaching start: the late Jim Harris, a coach for my brother Dave's wrestling team. After coming into the high school wrestling room as a college freshman and helping with some wrestling and mentoring, Coach Harris complimented me and said, "Tim, you did a great job with our team. Have you ever thought of going into coaching?" That spurred me to enter into the major of becoming a teacher and a coach. Thank you, Coach Harris, for the inspiration to have someone of your stature believe in me! I know you are looking down and pleased with what you did for me.

For those reading this book, always remember that it takes the help of others to reach a variety of goals. If you are as fortunate as I was, be sure to be a "Playing it Forward Coach", standing on your platform as a beacon of hope and positive energy for those young people you have the privilege of mentoring.

Timothy Law, author

References

Adrienne O'Neil, Shae E. Quirk, Siobhan Housden, Sharon L. Brennan, Lana J. Williams, Julie A. Pasco, Michael Berk, and Felice N. Jacka. 2014. "Relationship Between Diet and Mental Health in Children and Adolescents: A Systematic Review." *American Journal of Public Health* 104(10): e31–e42 (October). https://doi.org/10.2105/AJPH.2014.302110.

Ansorge, R. "Rest and recovery are critical for an athlete's physiological and psychological well-being," *UCHealth Today* (blog), uchealth. February 7, 2020. https://www.uchealth.org/today/rest-and-recovery-for-athletes-physiological-psychological-well-being/.

Bedosky, L. 2022. "What Is Breath Work—And Can It Help Your Sports Performance?" *Sports and Activity (blog)*, Nike. October 25, 2022. https://www.nike.com/a/how-breath-improves-performance#:~:text=Follow%20these%20steps%20from%20the,Strengthen%20your%20breathing%20muscles.

Bergland, C. 2023. "More Evidence That Exercise Can Alleviate Teenage Depression," *Depression* (blog), Psychology Today. January 6, 2023. https://www.psychologytoday.com/us/blog/the-athletes-way/202301/more-evidence-that-exercise-can-alleviate-teenage-depression.

Bomgren, L. 2023. "40-Minute Athletic High Intensity Workout." Nourish Move Love, April 6, 2023. https://www.nourishmovelove.com/40-minute-high-intensity-workout/.

Concordia University Chicago. 2018. "Practicing Mindfulness May Help Athletes Recover from Injury" Concordia University Chicago: Christ at the Center, July 12, 2018. https://exsci.cuchicago.edu/mindfulness-may-help-athletes-recover-injury/.

Creatitive. 2024. "Better Social Media Management Can Increase Athlete Sponsorship Opportunities." Creatitive. N.d. https://creatitive.com/social-media-management-boosts-athlete-sponsorship-opportunities/.

Davis, J. 2021. "Revisiting Growth Mindset as a Core Capacity of Sport Psychology." *AASP Blog* (blog), Applied Psychology. April 13, 2021. https://appliedsportpsych.org/blog/2021/04/revisiting-growth-mindset-as-a-core-capacity-of-sport-psychology/.

Ellison, J. 2020. "*Here's how the world has been shifting to* virtual sports: 8 big moments." Red Bull (blog), April 10, 2020. https://www.redbull.com/us-en/virtual-sports-best-moments.

Fry, A., and Dr. Rehman, A. 2023. "Sleep, Athletic Performance, and Recovery," *Physical Activity and Sleep* (blog), Sleep Foundation. December 13, 2023. https://www.sleepfoundation.org/physical-activity/athletic-performance-and-sleep.

Health Direct. 2023. "Health benefits of yoga and Pilates."healthdirect: free Australian health advice you can count on, June 2023. https://www.healthdirect.gov.au/health-benefits-of-yoga-and-pilates.

InnerDrive Team. 2024. "9 ways to use visualisation in sport," *Sport Psychology* (blog), InnerDrive. N.d. https://www.innerdrive.co.uk/blog/visualisation-in-sport/.

Lawrence W. Judge, David M. Bellar, Jennifer K. Popp, Bruce W. Craig, Makenzie A. Schoeff, Donald L. Hoover, Brian Fox, Brandon M. Kistler, and Ali M. Al-Nawaiseh. 2021. "Hydration to Maximize Performance and Recovery: Knowledge, Attitudes, and Behaviors Among Collegiate Track and Field Throwers." *Journal of Human Kinetics* 79: 111–122. https://doi.org/10.2478/hukin-2021-0065.

Lazzareschi, M. 2024. "The impacts of the COVID-19 pandemic on student athletes' mental health." *Wellfleet Student* (blog). N.d.

https://wellfleetstudent.com/behavioral-health/the-impacts-of-the-covid-19-pandemic-on-student-athletes-mental-health/.

Mahaffey, K. 2024. "Dynamic Warmups for Athletes: Exercises for Sports Performance," *Sports Performance* (blog), NASM. N.d. https://blog.nasm.org/dynamic-warm-ups-for-athletes-injury-prevention-and-sports-performance-benefits.

Mehta, K. 2020. "Inside The Mind Of Elite Athletes Who Become Outstanding Business Leaders" *Leadership Strategy* (blog), Forbes. October 14, 2020. https://www.forbes.com/sites/kmehta/2020/10/14/inside-the-mind-of-elite-athletes-who-become-outstanding-business-leaders/.

Nadja Walter, Lucie Nikoleizig, and Dorothee Alfermann. 2019. "Effects of Self-Talk Training on Competitive Anxiety, Self-Efficacy, Volitional Skills, and Performance: An Intervention Study with Junior Sub-Elite Athletes." *Sports (Basel)* 7(6): 148 (June). https://doi.org/10.3390/sports7060148.

National Institutes of Health. 2024. "Dietary Supplements for Exercise and Athletic Performance." National Institutes of Health: Office of Dietary Supplements, April 1, 2024. https://ods.od.nih.gov/factsheets/ExerciseAndAthleticPerformance-HealthProfessional/.

NSW Government. 2023. "The power of mental imagery." NSW Government: Office of Sport, May 2023. https://www.sport.nsw.gov.au/sites/default/files/2023-05/The-power-of-mental-imagery.pdf.

Nutrition News. 2023. "Understanding Sports Nutrition for Teens," Active Lifestlyes, Abbott. October 30, 2023. https://www.nutritionnews.abbott/healthy-living/active-lifestyle/understanding-sports-nutrition-for-teens/.

Orlando Treatment Solutions. 2023. *"Winning Strategies:* 15 Tips to Improve Mental Health for Athletes," (blog). *Orlando Treatment Solutions.* September 15, 2023. https://orlandotreatmentsolutions.com/15-tips-to-improve-mental-health-for-athletes/.

Peter Kass and Tyler E. Morrison. 2023. "The Impact of COVID-19 Restrictions on Youth Athlete Mental Health: A Narrative

Review." *Current Psychiatry Reports* 25(5): 193–199. https://doi.org/10.1007/s11920-023-01422-y.

Qinglei Wang, Nor Eeza Zainal Abidin, Mohd Salleh Aman, Nina Wang, Luhong Ma, and Pan Liu. 2024. "Cultural moderation in sports impact: exploring sports-induced effects on educational progress, cognitive focus, and social development in Chinese higher education." *BMC Psychology* 12: 89. February 22, 2024. https://doi.org/10.1186/s40359-024-01584-1.

Rosenbloom, C. 2021. "Teen Nutrition for Fall Sports," *Kids Eat Right* (blog), eatright.org. September 14, 2021. https://www.eatright.org/fitness/sports-and-athletic-performance/beginner-and-intermediate/teen-nutrition-for-fall-sports.

Sahen Gupta and Paul Joseph McCarthy. 2022. "The sporting resilience model: A systematic review of resilience in sports performers." *Frontiers in Psychology* 13: 1003053 (December). https://doi.org/10.3389/fpsyg.2022.1003053.

Sifan Wang, Lin Chen, Hailiang Ran, Yusan Che, Die Fang, Hao Sun, Junwei Peng, Xuemeng Liang, and Yuanyuan Xiao. 2022. "Depression and anxiety among children and adolescents pre and post COVID-19: A comparative meta-analysis." *Front Psychiatry* 13: 917552 (August). https://doi.org/10.3389/fpsyt.2022.917552.

Soller, A. 2020. *"The Stay-at-Home Athlete: Build Your Home-Based Athletic Performance Program." NIFS Healthy Living Blog* (blog), NIFS. April 23, 2020. https://www.nifs.org/blog/the-stay-at-home-athlete-building-your-home-based-athletic-performance-program.

Steel Supplements. *2020.* "The Definitive Home Workout Plan for Teenagers," The Steel Library (blog). Steel Supplements. September 6, 2020. https://steelsupplements.com/blogs/steel-blog/the-definitive-home-workout-plan-for-teenagers.

Untapped Learning. 2024. "Importance of Mentorship for Student-Athletes," *Untapped* (blog). N.d. https://untappedlearning.com/importance-of-mentorship-for-student-athletes/#:~:text=Studies%20from%20the%20US%20Department,more%20than%20just%20the%20athlete.

Von Moltke, D. 2022. "Science of Breath Work: Breathing for Athletes," (blog). *Blayze*. November 14, 2022. https://blayze.io/blog/general/the-science-of-breathing-for-athletes.

Warner, I. 2020. "5 Keys for a Strong Transition From High School Sports to College Athlete," *Sports, Stack*. August, 14, 2020. https://www.stack.com/a/5-keys-for-successfully-transitioning-from-high-school-sports-to-college-athlete/.

Watson, D. 2023. "Mental Health in Teen Athletes," *Healthy Living* (blog), healthychildren.org. August 16, 2023. https://www.healthychildren.org/English/healthy-living/sports/Pages/mental-health-in-teen-athletes.aspx.

Yeager, A. 2022. "How mindfulness-based training can give elite athletes a mental edge." *Psychology* (blog), Science News. January 26, 2022. https://www.sciencenews.org/article/athlete-mental-health-mindfulness-psychology-elite-olympics.

Made in the USA
Coppell, TX
26 February 2025

46453727R00069